I want to extend a special thank you to the over 100 marketers, developers, designers, salespeople, and executives who have been instrumental in giving me input and feedback on this book. I am inspired daily by the incredible work that is being done by these world-class businesspeople, and I hope this book accurately reflects the brilliance I see inside of you all.

This book was edited by Hank Greene and designed by Lee Eisenbarth. Both have been incredible partners in this endeavor and I'm really proud of their work.

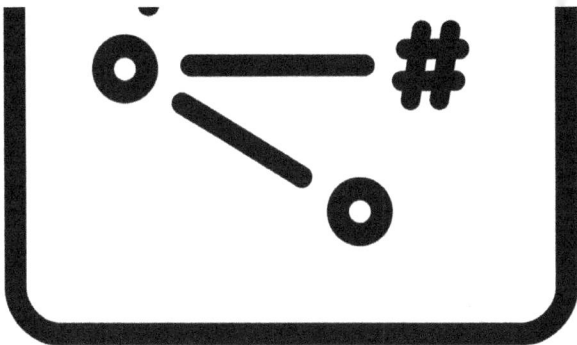

THE FUTURE-PROOF
MARKETING
PLAYBOOK

TIM HICKLE

Table of Contents

About The Author

Tim Hickle is a speaker, marketer, author, and singer of very silly songs. Based out of Indianapolis, Tim has spent his career helping businesses of all shapes and sizes improve their presence in their market.

When he's not talking about marketing, Tim enjoys drinking craft beer, watching the Indiana Hoosiers, and guilting people into laughing at his jokes.

About This Book

This book was written for marketers at any level who want to view their job through a more strategic framework. Each chapter includes action items that you can implement today, but this book is intentionally light on marketing tactics. Instead, this book challenges you to zoom out and focus on the strategic value of each of your marketing activities.

I intentionally designed the book with a wide top margin for note taking, so please don't hesitate to jot, doodle, and dog ear! In case you run into a piece of jargon that you're not familiar with, I've also included an alphabetized glossary in the back of the book.

Happy reading!

Tim

"Champions aren't made in the gyms. Champions are made from something they have deep inside them — a desire, a dream, a vision of their digital marketing strategy."

— Muhammad Ali, probably

I'm Tim Hickle, and this is my playbook to help you build a sustainable marketing ecosystem.

Throughout my career, I've worked with every type of business—from Mom and Pop shops, to publicly traded companies. I've worked with startups, scale-ups, and end-ups. I've worked in high-tech and low-tech industries. I've worked in-house. I've worked in an agency. And throughout this time marketing in so many different industries for clients with a variety of needs, I've seen one problem plaguing my occupational field above all else:

Shortsightedness.

Far too many marketers look at the digital landscape of 2017 and think that "long-term" planning means trying to find the loophole in the new Google algorithm update before their competition does.

The truth about digital marketing, though, is that it's a game. And like any game, you need a set of strategies that will help you react to the changing circumstances of the playing field.

Great coaches don't take pride in their ability to get one play right, or even win one game—they take pride in their ability to win sustainably in a variety of circumstances, with a team and a mindset ready to tackle anything that the opposition throws at them. Your digital marketing strategy should be no different. If your marketing department's primary focus is at the tactical level—optimizing email open rate, driving more traffic to your blog, or even... *going viral* (puke)—you're missing the bigger picture and falling behind your peers; peers who have focused on building sustainable business strategies into their marketing efforts.

Part of the issue is that too many marketers are mistaking changes in technology for changes in underlying business. On the contrary, just like any great sport, the basic principles of the marketing game haven't changed. The truth is, about 80 percent of this book is industry principles and fundamentals that experts have been espousing for years. But just as new players, rules, or styles of play force even the best sports minds to adjust, so too must the best minds of the marketing world take these traditional ideas and fit them into a modernized game.

This playbook is broken down into the three main facets of a successful sports organization:

1. Your "owner philosophy"—or the core set of values upon which you'll build your winning team.

2. Your "in-game coaching"—or the approach you'll take to your day-to-day operations within your marketing and sales department.

3. Your "GM vision"—or the way you'll "future-proof" your marketing to assure that your team is still winning five years from now.

What you'll find in these pages isn't the cheapest way to do business, nor is it the secret to generating the "fastest results." You'll have to make some sacrifices in order to implement it effectively, and it'll take time. Ask any General Manager in professional sports, and they'll tell you that short-term planning may get you wins, but time, patience, and effort will get you championships.

Those are the terms. So if you value virality over substance, quick hits over sustainability, and the trick play over the development of a consistent run game that will open up the passing attack (don't worry, we'll get there), then put this book down.

If, however, you're ready to learn my game... turn the page, and let's start playing.

Part 1

BUILDING YOUR FRANCHISE:

Establishing a Winning Digital Foundation

"Confidence comes from being prepared with a great, attainable marketing vision."

— John Wooden, I guess

Every successful team starts with a successful foundation. Sure, jumping right in and figuring out your next blog series may seem like a more fun way to get results today, but taking the time in the offseason to put together a solid plan of attack for the upcoming year is a must for any championship team— and so too must it be for your marketing department.

In this section, we'll focus on how you can use some basic, high-level marketing principles to build your franchise into a marketing juggernaut.

Strategists vs. Tacticians: Why You Need a Playbook

Due to the rapid rise of technological innovation in the marketing industry, today's marketing landscape is extremely diverse. Consequently, the types of personalities attracted to marketing today are more diverse than ever. While the Mad Men days have long past, there are still plenty of wanna-be Don Drapers hanging around the industry, but there are also tons of lean startup guys, corporate evangelists, brand ambassadors, technophobes, technophiles, guerrilla marketers, growth-hackers, and "storytellers."

Despite this massive diversity in personality type, I've noticed one clear line in the sand that separates the most successful marketers in the world from those who are constantly playing catch up—deliberate strategy.

On one side of this line, you have the marketers who I refer to as "tacticians." Some of them are incredibly talented at what they do, but their primary course of action resides at the tactical level. They might be really talented at designing ads, managing PPC campaigns, or writing copy—all three of which are incredible skills to have—but they struggle to zoom out and see the larger picture beyond the tactics. They approach marketing by thinking about what they want to do, like "launch a direct mail campaign" or "create engaging content for our Twitter followers."

On the other side of this line, you have the marketers who I call "strategists." Some of them are talented at the tactical level, some aren't, but they know how to hire talented tacticians. They view all marketing through the lens of its desired outcome. They're constantly balancing cost vs. benefit in their heads, and they're not afraid to cut corners when the numbers don't quite add up. They know when to call the "A+ creative" play, and they know when they can afford to dial it back. They know what aspects of their marketing need to be world class and what aspects can afford to be B or C level work.

They're not artisans—they're competitors, and they know what it takes to win at the game of business. These are the people who are winning in today's competitive landscape, and they're leveraging strategies that position them to win in the future, regardless of what technological changes come their way.

My goal with this book is to shine a light on these strategists and teach you how you can join their ranks. I want your marketing efforts to be future-proof. Instead of chasing success on another social media channel or a Google algorithm change, I want you to build a strategic framework, under which every activity is deliberately defined.

Now, I can't undersell the importance of tactical success, but if you only focus on tactical success you'll miss how these tactics fit into the larger game your playing. Football isn't about how far your quarterback can throw—it's about how his passes line up with his receivers, allowing the team to score more touchdowns, and that is your central mission.

It's important to have a broader view of your marketing's strategic impact if you want to build a framework that won't break under the pressure of changing platforms, buyer's' preferences, or staff makeup.

So let's simplify the game a bit. Stop thinking of marketing as the series of little ideas, adjustments or strategies, and instead find the central mission you're looking to accomplish:

Marketing is about finding ways to communicate and connect your product to the everyday lives of your target market.

As such, any organization that takes marketing seriously should do three things effectively:

- **Branding** – Crafts and positions your brand awareness and products competitively in the targeted marketplace.

- **Lead Generation** - Builds and maintains a strong pipeline of active leads that result in sales conversions.

- **Sales Support** - Optimizes your sales process for conversion, ranging from UX/UI optimization to direct customer service.

That's all we're doing. Every function of your marketing department should fit into one of those categories. Depending on the makeup of your team, you may focus on one category substantially more than the others—and that's okay!

The ratio doesn't need to be 33% all around. Some organizations will prioritize lead generation above branding, while others will focus on optimizing their sales process before they want to build a lead gen pipeline. There's no wrong way to prioritize these items, but there is a minimum distribution of focus, below which you're not marketing strategically.

Something you'll notice throughout this book is that I have a golden ratio: 60-30-10. This balance allows you to have one clear focus, a clear backup, and a tertiary option that can build over time. While I recommend that organizations build their teams and priorities around this ratio, there's also nothing wrong with 50-25-25, 33-33-33, or 80-10-10. The whole point is to simply ensure that your department is balanced enough to give three aspects of your marketing approach an effective level of focus and effort.

If, however, you're not allocating at least ten percent of your marketing budget, headcount, and efforts to all three of these functions, you're doing yourself a disservice. I've worked with organizations that focus every marketing dollar on lead generation. This strategy works for a while before ultimately falling apart, and the same goes for only focusing on branding, or sales support.

Diversification is as important to your marketing strategy as it is to developing an effective offensive strategy in football. You can't just run the same play over and over again, because if that play fails you need to be able to run something else.

Remember, *marketing is about finding ways to communicate and connect your product to the everyday lives of consumers.*

This is something that the strategists understand, and it's the reason that they're going to be far more successful than their tactician counterparts. This game isn't just branding, just lead generation, and just sales support—it's the way all of these things intertwine to help you accomplish your endgame, leading you to victory.

Why Focus on Future-Proofing?

On the surface, the strategists and tacticians look very similar. They both create marketing plans, they both measure similar key performance indicators, and they both use very similar marketing channels to accomplish their goals. The big difference isn't in their actions, it's in their attitudes, and in a constantly changing tech landscape strategists are the ones who will come out ahead.

The strategists, you see, understand something that tacticians don't: the only way to prevent technological change from damaging your marketing efforts is to build a future-proof plan that can withstand anything that gets thrown at it.

Unfortunately, too many people in the industry don't see it this way. With so much change happening constantly within the industry, I get constant pushback from heads of organizations large and small that don't understand why they'd focus on marketing efforts beyond the next six months. They want a sleek website, more leads, and whatever key performance indicators they're looking to achieve *today*. Who cares about regulations from tech giants?

If you've ever had a domain blacklisted by Google, you know it can be a nightmare. Unfortunately, if recent trends persist, penalties and blacklisting are going to be far more pervasive in the coming years, and it's not for reasons you may expect.

Google is making changes – not just to search, but also to their entire suite of products. This could have massive ramifications across the digital marketing community. Consequently, most marketers are likely to get blindsided in the coming years by ranking factors they're not even thinking about.

Strategists have nothing to fear, but I see a terrifying future on the horizon for tacticians—one in which you won't be able to overcompensate for lack of organic search traffic with PPC, social media, or email... because Google will find you.

So, how do we build a marketing ecosystem that Google can't break?

League Scouting Report: The Current Digital Marketing Landscape

Before we get too far ahead of ourselves thinking about the future, let's take a quick look at the present state of digital marketing today, and the new metric ready to completely change the industry...

User Behavior: Digital Marketing's Newest MVP

Remember the good ol' days of backlinks and PageRank? Well, I hope you took pictures to save those memories because Google's grown up a lot in the past few years. While quality and quantity of backlinks still matter for SEO, Google has increased the importance of user behavior data in their search algorithm significantly over the past few years.

This has placed a greater emphasis on how users *interact* with your site and content, instead of simply viewing clicks as the be-all, end-all. If users spend more time on your site, and engage with more of your content, your site will climb the ranks of Google's algorithm. If not, you run the risk of becoming *that guy* in every pickup basketball game who chucks up a three every time you pass to him.

You hate playing with that guy, and so does Google.

What does all this mean? If people like your content, you can punch out of your weight class. If people hate your content, you can't do enough digital PR to overcome it.

For those with high bounce rates or low click through rates on SERPs, this should scare you. Google's results are systematically weeding out people exactly like you, so it's time to step up your content and user experience game to meet the new demand. You either update your site and content to keep with the times, or your search presence dies.

Search, Email, Display, and Social: How it All Connects

Unlike Panda and Penguin, these recent Google updates favoring user behavior data haven't lived in a vacuum—they're being reflected in Gmail's inbox, Google's display advertising, and even social media.

User behavior is becoming pervasive throughout the digital ecosystem. If your data is sending the wrong signals you won't just drop out of search results—you'll begin showing up in fewer inboxes, and will have to pay more for digital ads than your competitors.

Everywhere you turn, platforms are turning their main focus to the following metrics:

- Click through rate

- Bounce rate

- Time on page

- Pages/Session

- Pogo-Sticking

If you're not watching these rates and keeping an eye on industry averages, you're putting yourself in a very dangerous position moving forward—and not just for the reasons you'd expect back in 2013…

Cross-Channel Penalization, or, Why the 3-Point Shot Changed Basketball Forever

In 1967, the American Basketball Association introduced a new rule to its game: players who hit a shot from behind a line placed 25 feet from the basket would receive *three* points for their team, instead of the two points traditionally awarded from anywhere on the court up until that point.

Many criticized the rule as a passing fad, and the more popular basketball league at the time, the National Basketball Association—or NBA—dismissed it as nothing more than a publicity stunt, vowing it would never be introduced to their league.

You can probably guess what happened next. Upon its introduction in the NBA in 1979, the 3-point shot became one of the most important strategic aspects of the game. Today, it affects ball movement, defensive strategy, offensive efficiency, and most analytics indicate that in the modern NBA, a team's three-point percentage is one of the most important indicators of their overall success.

In digital marketing, just like in basketball, one small rule change affects everything else around it.

Today, user behavior data is siloed. Your high bounce rate is only affecting your SEO efforts. If you think even a few years into the future, however, it becomes very easy to paint a more pessimistic picture.

If Google is already penalizing you for bad user experience across all of their channels, why would they stop there? Why not share that data cross-channel? It doesn't take much imagination to picture a reality where getting too many spam reports would result in lower organic search results and higher CPC on advertising efforts.

This is why it's extremely important to take this seriously today. If you wait until Google starts this cross-channel penalizing, you'll risk your marketing efforts becoming obsolete at best, and permanently stifled at worst.

Creating Your Future-Proof Gameplan

Like I said in my introduction, future-proofing your marketing efforts won't be easy.

You'll have to spend more money on your website. You'll have to think more deliberately about your strategy. You have to imagine the absolute worst-case scenario, and then you have to prepare for something even worse than that.

The good news, though, is that this game can be won. Looking towards the future with your marketing isn't about trying to "outsmart" Google or find a loophole in their algorithm—it's about coming up with a consistent, malleable, big-picture approach that can be adjusted to the latest in the digital marketing landscape.

Building the Team: Filling Your Roster with Digital Marketing All-Stars

Now that you understand where the league sits currently, it's time to stock your team with the players poised to take your marketing efforts to the next level.

When it comes to talent acquisition, many believe that in today's hiring ecosystem, the most effective decisions are the ones that focus on the most specific candidates with the most specific skillsets, much like filling a football roster. After all, with so much to focus on, what better way to ensure that you're firing on all cylinders than to hire people with unique expertise to handle each portion of your marketing, right?

Wrong.

Let's say you're hiring an in-house PPC-specialist. As you create this role, you have the choice between writing a job description that's 100% PPC-focused or writing a job description that is predominantly PPC-focused while still giving this prospective employee exposure to other aspects of the marketing team.

I would opt for description number two every time for a few reasons:

1. It's a heck of a lot easier to find a good PPC person who has a diverse skillset than to find the best PPC person in your world.

2. It's a lot easier to attract highly-talented candidates with future management potential if you have a diverse job description that allows them to broaden their experience.

3. Specialists get sniped. Period. I've never seen a highly-trained specialist who doesn't get headhunted weekly.

4. Specialists generally cost more with much lower potential upside.

5. Let's say another employee leaves and this candidate has to shift over to take over some of their responsibilities. Would you rather have a complete novice or someone with some experience?

6. Specialists lead to silos. Silos lead to communication breakdowns. Communication breakdowns kill teams.

All this is to say that when you're staffing your marketing department, don't staff like a football team, staff like a fútbol team (or soccer team for all you American tossers). Find a group of well-rounded candidates who, though they may have specific strengths, have diverse enough skillsets to balance your team's attack.

Remember our focus on branding, lead generation, and sales support? Those three categories are integral to your success, and it's important that everyone on your team understands all three at an intimate level.

The Art of Talent Scouting: Job Descriptions and Meeting Your Company's Needs

Building a future-proof team means building a team that can't destroy itself. If you're hiring the best talent that you can find, you're likely to have some of your best people poached. That's okay. It's your job to be prepared for that. That's why I recommend drafting the best player available instead of drafting for a position.

That's not to say that your employees shouldn't have a clear focus. They should, but that focus should be balanced with a well-rounded understanding of the rest of your operation. A good example of this might look something like this:

- 60% Lead Generation. This is their specialty. Every responsibility for this aspect of the role should have to do with lead generation.

- 30% Sales Support. This is their secondary focus. Every responsibility in this section should have to do with sales support.

- 10% Branding. This is tertiary. They should get some exposure and if they show promise, you can always add more to their plate.

Taking this approach to your job listing will not only help you attract the best job seekers—as young talent is generally looking to branch out with a more varied day-to-day work experience—it also hedges your bets when your team changes. If you lose a sales support stud, you'll have a handful of talented, potential-filled team members ready and willing to step up in a pinch.

Plus, having a team with diversified tools fosters greater communication and collaboration amongst your team. Even if you don't necessarily *need* someone in a lead gen role to help out with branding work, it benefits your team to collaborate on projects.

The Team Philosophy: Your "Big Picture" Approach

So, you've assembled a team ready to work together and revolutionize your company's marketing efforts. But before you hit the field and get to work, consider your first major organizational question:

What is your marketing department's management and project implementation structure going to look like?

The workplace has changed more in the last 20 years than it did in the century prior, and it's undoubtedly going to continue changing much more in the years to come. Technology is facilitating more remote work and rapid communication than ever. That's making the job market incredibly competitive, and if you want to build a winning team, you need to be a "player's GM." You need to know how to coach your team in a way that gets them excited and motivated, or your best talent will go elsewhere.

Because of these changes, management structures are changing, and in the marketing space, this is extremely problematic. The entire advertising industry was built around the traditional "stand and deliver" model, but as the tech boom hit its second wave and The Lean Startup entered the public lexicon, lean marketing became the king of the block.

Both sides think that theirs is the only way, and both sides are dead wrong. In fact, the only way to build a truly future-proof marketing strategy at the organizational and staff management level is to eschew both methodologies for a middle road.

Top-Down Marketing: Why Stand-and-Deliver Fails

This is by far the most common methodology in corporate America, and for good reason. It's been tested for decades and it's always worked.

The concept seems logical—your CMO or your ad agency goes into their secluded room, high in their ivory tower, and they emerge with an annual marketing strategy. This plan isn't written in ink; it's carved in stone.

This is our playbook. This is how we win.

This method worked extremely well when the world operated at the speed of television and radio ads. You could get away with a rigid game plan when you only had to contend with a few channels and your competition or customer couldn't shift at a moment's notice.

The problem is, as markets matured and technology ballooned, the game got much more difficult. Now, if you're still running the same plays in October as you were running in January, you're unlikely to get the results you need in order to top your competition.

This was the way of the past, but the Mad Men days are over and no Draper-esque tagline will sustain your marketing efforts for a full year. Stand-and-deliver marketing efforts are the past, and they're not future-proof.

Bottom-Up Marketing: Why Lean Marketing Fails

In a lot of forward-thinking industries, companies have begun to implement lessons from books like *The Lean Startup* into every aspect of their business model.

The idea is simple: build your minimum viable product (or MVP) and go to market as soon as possible, letting market feedback dictate product development. Essentially—go into the game with a strategy for victory, and make all the adjustments you need at halftime. This will cut your upfront costs and prevent you from building features that the market doesn't care about.

Unfortunately, this approach—often called "growth hacking"—usually misses the forest for the trees.

From a product development perspective, this has proven to be an incredibly effective methodology, and there are definitely marketing lessons to be learned from this approach. For example, the "go to market quickly and test" methodology is extremely effective at testing new and emerging channels.

The key fact that "growth hackers" forget, though, is that your marketing strategy is much more comprehensive than running some PPC ads—it's a holistic approach that needs to be thought out and committed to so that you can have a map for change when those changes need to be made.

Think of it this way: you can make halftime adjustments in the middle of an individual game, but you can't suddenly reverse all of the team-wide things you focused on during training camp without losing the trust of your players, the organization, and your fans.

There are a few core reasons that "lean marketing" fails in the real world, and they reflect some important business fundamentals:

- **If you don't have time to do it right, when do you have time to do it again? -** So you got a logo on Fiverr because you're on a tight budget. Great. When do you have time to pay someone for a real logo? Do it right or don't do it.

- **You'll end up re-doing a lot of work -** Even if you do get around to completing tasks after the market testing, often you'll find yourself just redoing work that would have just been simpler to do right the first time around.

- **Rebrands strain brand trust and equity -** If you believe in the idea of brand trust and brand equity at all, you get a very limited number of rebrands. I've seen far too many companies say, "Oh, we'll just go to market with this name and then rebrand later." That can work, but you only get one get out of jail free card. If you change your name and logo every two years, you lose trust from the marketplace and any equity you built before.

- **Building assets requires quality work -** I'm too young to use the "They don't make things like they used to" line, but if you want to build marketing assets that continue to drive results months and years after you paid for them, you have to build them right the first time.

Lean marketing can be effective in some circumstances, but if you rely on lean marketing to build your brand or create assets that will have a lasting impact on your business, you'll fail. Lean marketing efforts may be the present, but they're not future-proof.

The Compromise: Agile Marketing and Your Business

Both stand-and-deliver and lean marketing methodologies have merit. There are times when each are appropriate, but neither strategy alone is capable of crafting an effective marketing strategy in the 21st century.

The compromise is to find the balance in your marketing efforts by utilizing the best of both worlds. You need both the structure of a game plan and the ability to make in-game adjustments.

This approach is known as *agile marketing.*

Agile marketing gets its inspiration from the world of software development. Much like lean marketing, it is build around a fast-paced, iterative approach, but it also mixes in a healthy dose of central planning.

The basic gist is this: take the entire scope of everything that you want your marketing team to do and break those pieces into "points." The idea is to measure points by total working hours, but a point is just a unit of measurement, used to simplify the planning process. You can make a "point" worth any number of working hours, or days, as is convenient for you and your team.

Some people make one "point" equal to one day's worth of work, some make one "point" worth one hour of work. I personally recommend making one point worth four working hours, but it really just comes down to your personal preference.

Next, you'll organize all of your marketing activities into "sprints." A sprint is just a period of time, made up of a set amount of the "points" you've already established, in which you are going to be focused on the work that you outline in your sprint plan. Some people plan for sprints to be one week, some people make sprints a whole month. Personally, I prefer two week sprints because they allow you to react quickly to changes in priorities while also providing you enough time to accomplish a lot in each sprint.

Now that you know how many points you have in a sprint, all you need to do is fill in the blanks with activities.

This methodology is both resilient and adaptive. It gives your team freedom and flexibility to shift their priorities as the competitive landscape changes, while also providing you with enough centralized control to keep everyone on-message and marching in the right direction.

The best part of agile marketing? It's extremely easy to implement and it can be broken down into three component parts: Sprint planning, sprinting, and a sprint retrospective. Let's walk through each of these components.

Sprint Planning

Everything starts with sprint planning. Think of this like your week's practice leading up to the big weekend game—it's all about putting forth your game plan, and making sure everyone on your team knows their assignment going in.

Sprint planning starts with identifying your key stakeholders and a primary point of contact for each. For example, let's say you need to focus on the following:

- Corporate brand identity with your CEO as your main point of contact

- Sales support and lead generation with your VP of Sales as your main point of contact

- Product marketing with your VP of Product as your main point of contact

- Legal compliance with your lawyer as your main point of contact

Assign each of those stakeholders to a member of your team. They own that relationship and it's their responsibility beforehand to have a solid understanding of what that stakeholder needs throughout the sprint. If anyone else from a stakeholder's department comes to you for help, run it through your main point of contact.

The most important part of this process is to understand your priorities. Make sure everyone on your team is making a list of tasks in priority order for the stakeholder—this will prevent confusion and frustration later.

Each of these points of contact will get a percentage of your points dedicated to them each sprint. This percentage will be consistent every sprint, and it will be determined on a quarterly basis. So, for example, let's say that at the beginning of the quarter, you sit down with your executive team and all key stakeholders. You decide in that meeting that 25% of your points will be dedicated to corporate brand identity. That means that, every sprint, approximately 25% of your points will go to that key stakeholder.

Depending on your company's priorities, this could vary dramatically by organization, and it will probably vary from quarter-to-quarter, but it's important to keep this as consistent as possible. If you're giving the product team ten percent of your time one sprint and half of your time the next sprint, other departments and stakeholders are bound to get upset.

Once you know how your points will be divided among your stakeholders, it's time to assign point values to each task. Your first few sprint planning sessions will be hard and will take some time to perfect, but they'll get easier over time.

Now, when you're figuring out how many points a particular task should take (or "point values"), there are a few different ways you can go about it. My personal favorite method is to use a deck of cards; each card representing a particular point value that corresponds to the amount of time a task may take. You list off a task, your team discusses it, and then everyone plays a card at the same time that represents the number of points they think it will take. You can use a regular deck of cards, or just Google "Sprint Planning Poker" to find a deck more uniquely suited to the task.

At this point you should have all the pieces in place to properly plan your sprint. You have established:

- How many points you have over the course of your sprint.

- A breakdown of how many points you're planning to use on each stakeholder.

- What needs every key stakeholder has, and what needs take priority.

- A listing of how many points each item is worth.

This should put you in a position to easily assign items and have your team knock them out. It also helps you prioritize items when someone swoops in at the midnight hour to request something "urgent."

In this instance, you can just respond, "I'd be happy to get that done. Which of these items my team has assigned for delivery to your department this sprint would you like knocked off our list?" This approach makes everything consistent, manageable, and keeps you honest on how much bandwidth your team has.

Sprinting

It's game time; hop into the sprint. To make this process easier, I recommend getting a physical board (analog, I know) that walks through the following stages:

- To-Do

- In Progress

- Awaiting Approval

- Done

Print off sheets of paper with every activity you're tackling during this sprint and tape them up in the "To-Do" section at the beginning of the sprint. Every morning, have a quick standup meeting where your team can move over items to "In-Progress," "Awaiting Approval," or "Done."

During this meeting, make sure to ask every team member if they have any roadblocks standing in their way. This can help you diagnose problems before the sprint is over, so there are no surprises.

Depending on your level of sophistication, you can get extremely granular with your analysis. Some people create burn-down charts, while others use software to measure team members' productivity over time. Feel free to make this process as complicated as you're comfortable with, but remember that it doesn't *have* to be complex if you don't want it to be—it can be as simple as a white board and some paper.

Sprint Retrospective

After your sprint is over, it's time for your post-game press conference—a moment to sit and review the process before jumping back into your next round of sprint planning. During the retrospective, you want to get everyone on your team involved and active.

Make sure you cover the following:

- **Show and Tell -** Have everyone on your team show the end results from their sprint. This will help your team understand what everyone does and see the end result of a campaign, as often times people only see the component parts they're working on.

- **Lessons Learned -** Have everyone talk about things that they learned throughout the sprint, and offer advice and encouragement to their teammates.

- **What Did I Do Wrong? -** Have every member of your team talk about things that they did wrong. Don't let this devolve into finger pointing. Keep this focused and, as the leader, make sure you're encouraging everyone on your team to meet this process with positivity.

This meeting will take awhile and it can get heavy at times. Take a break between each section of the meeting and do something light that your team will enjoy. Some people do retrospectives over beers, while some watch cat videos between sections. You know your team, so you'll know what will work best for them—just make sure to find something that will help them unwind and rest their brains for a bit.

Finally, given everything you just learned, plan your next sprint!

That's all there is to agile marketing. If you can implement these steps, you can build a marketing department that's built to weather any storm, and pivot on a dime. For more information on Agile Management, I'd recommend *Scrum: a Breathtakingly Brief and Agile Introduction*, by Chris Sims.

So, now that we've built your team, let's build out the final, but piece of your digital marketing foundation.

Building a Resilient Website

There are only a few things in this world that make me cry. In fact, basketball documentaries and companies stuck on the website treadmill are about it. It saddens me to know how many companies redo their website, top-to-bottom, every 18 months. Not only is this expensive and wasteful, it's annoying to your users.

Unfortunately, though, this is what cheap business owners get. If you hire a cut-rate vendor or try to do it yourself in-house with someone who has never built a website before, you'll come out the other end looking great... for a few months.

Soon things will start breaking. Next, design trends will make your site look antiquated. Then, a competitor will launch something new and flashy, and now you're rebuilding your website all over again, because you need to keep up with the Joneses... but there's a better way.

The foundation of a future-proof digital presence is a resilient website.

That's not to say that your website won't change over time—change is inevitable. If you build it right, however, your website will grow with you.

Staying Ahead of Technical Requirements

Technological change is inevitable, but just because something changes doesn't mean your website has to break. You can build a house of brick instead of straw. There's no rule against it, it costs you less in the long run, and it keeps you safe from big, bad wolves.

So how do you do it? *By hiring a UX designer.*

It's extremely important that we draw a line in the sand between a UX designer and a graphic designer. A UX (User Experience) designer is focused on how people use your website. Their primary focus is use cases and delivering information in a timely manner. They usually don't care what things look like—they care about how they work.

When you're in the early stages of the web development process, looks aren't important—what's important is *message, meaning, and purpose.* Why do people access your website? What are they looking to accomplish? What are you looking to communicate? A graphic designer, by their very definition, cannot help you answer these questions.

It's for this reason that I usually recommend working with an agency. If you have a solid eye for messaging, can hire a killer UX designer, can hire a great graphic designer, and can hire at least one top-performing front end developer, then you should do it in-house.

If not, you should either hire an agency or completely cheap out and get a Squarespace site. Whether you're looking for an agency or a UX designer, however, it's important that you know how to evaluate their work effectively.

Here are some key indicators that a website isn't resilient enough to deal with future technological changes:

- **It's not resilient to changes in technology today**—e.g. not responsive on mobile devices; not built for "in-between" screens, like tablets; has broken elements on various modern or antiquated browsers; stretches or distorts when you change the size of your browser window.

- **It's not resilient to changes in content**—e.g. it requires headlines that are over or under a certain character count for the design to work; it's heavily reliant on having the best photography or videography to look good; it doesn't lend itself to changing needs within the website.

- **It's not able to grow with your needs**—e.g. you can't spin up landing pages easily without calling your development team; you can't make significant content or site architecture changes.

- **Its performance is average**—e.g. it scores in the yellow or red section of Google Pagespeed Insights; it shows middling scores on speed checkers like Pingdom; it has render-blocking Javascript, instead of loading Javascript asynchronously.

Over time, as technology grows, fast sites get faster and slow sites get slower. Resilient websites are built with progressive enhancement in mind.

Building a Website Conducive to Change

If you want to build a future-proof website, you don't want to focus on the end result, because that, by its very nature, will change.

Instead, you want to focus on giving yourself the building blocks to design not just the website you want today, but any website that you may want in the future. This is called "modular design," and it's an incredible resource when building a website that can grow with you through the years.

Before you sit down to wireframe a single page, it's important to consider important UX questions, such as...

- What do you want your ideal users to do when they show up on your homepage?

- When the average user shows up your website, how are they finding you, what do they want to do, and why do they want this particular experience?

- What do the different users who visit your site look like? (This is an area where persona dossiers can be extremely useful)

- What other sites do these individuals like to get information from, and why are they drawn there?

- What common "use cases" exist across your website?

These are incredibly important questions to consider as you design major pages on your website. Design preferences may change regularly, but use cases rarely do. Usually, your target market is going to utilize your website in the same way for years, with very little change. A good UX designer should know how to ask these questions, find the answers, and design a website that solves your users' problems.

This should result in things like high-level wireframes built around primary messages, information, and actions. Think of these like a blueprint for your house: it's really easy to re-paint your house to make it nice, and it's pretty easy to knock down a non load-bearing wall to open up your living room—but it's really hard and expensive to add another wing on the back.

All you need to know at this stage is that the foundation is secure and that you won't want to add another wing.

Avoiding Design Fads

When designing a website, it's not all about technical specifications—you also need a keen eye on the website's look and feel.

A common concern I hear from clients is that they don't want their new, modern, sleek (not to mention expensive) website to be outdated in a year. Design trends and fads are a serious concern if you're trying to build something truly future-proof, so how do you avoid designing a *trendy* website, and instead design a *lasting* website?

This is where UX plays an important role. The look and feel of your website is not your website, just like a coat of paint isn't your house. You can always change imagery, colors, and copy. You can even alter layout without too much hassle!

What you need, however, is a website that is conducive to these changes and a systematized approach to making these changes at scale.

Remember to always keep in mind what it is your customers are looking to do when they arrive at your website. Don't worry so much about keeping up with what your main competitors' websites look like, but rather always have an eye towards how they function.

The more time you spend stressing over making your color scheme pop, the less time you'll have to understand how the UX of your website can easily convert users into sales.

Building a System that Keeps Your Website Current

From here, you'll design and launch your new website. Congratulations! Unfortunately, after about 12 to 18 months people will start complaining.

Your sales staff will complain because your site doesn't look as modern as your competitor's newly re-launched website. Your product team will complain because you haven't built out a section talking about their new gizmo's product specs.

This is where agile marketing can be a lifesaver.

Instead of waiting for requests to come in, proactively do a competitive analysis of your marketplace once a quarter. Review this analysis in your sprint planning meeting at the beginning of the next quarter, and assess changes that you want to make over the next few sprints.

This should include things like:

- **Performance metrics -** Pingdom analysis, Google Pagespeed Insights, etc.

- **Vanity metrics -** Alexa Ranking, Domain Authority, Estimated Monthly Traffic, Social Media Following.

- **Aesthetic choices –** Use screenshots of your competition's website to note what they do well, what they do poorly, and what you want to capitalize on.

This puts you in the driver's seat both in your company and in your industry, so you can make small changes over time to keep your website current with emerging trends.

Taking Stock of Your Newest Franchise

Congratulations! You're now running a franchise! You've built a team that can pivot and adjust with ease, and you've built assets that can weather the storm of technological change.

The bad news? You still haven't played a game yet.

Throughout Part 1, we've looked at the foundational approach to a successful digital marketing department. We've assessed the central mission of marketing, talked about the necessary roster of players whose diverse skillsets will allow you to succeed, discussed how to put a high-level system in place to help manage your team, and looked at how to create a future-proof website to build your efforts on.

Now, it's time to gather up your coaching staff, lock yourself away in your office, and design the in-game playbook you'll use to win at the highest level.

Play Calls - Building Your Franchise

Here's a list of things you can do today to start building your franchise.

- Document how you want to diversify your marketing efforts between branding, lead generation, and sales support.

- Perform a site audit of your website and your three biggest competitors.

- Document a strategy for implementing agile management with your team.

Part 2

CRAFTING YOUR GAME PLAN:

Coaching Your Marketing to Success

"The difference between a successful person and others is not a lack of strength, not a lack of knowledge, but rather in a lack of scalability in their digital marketing strategy."

— Vince Lombardi, maybe

You've built your franchise, picked your players, figured out how you'll balance top-down and bottom-down organizational approaches, and now you're ready to hit the field and start sprinting towards marketing glory.

But before you can do that, you need to figure out how your marketing department will work together over the course of the season to create a balanced, winning attack.

In this section, we'll cover the three major foci your marketing will have to take into consideration, and discuss how you'll need each one to help you win.

Defense: A Winning Brand

Every championship team begins with a stalwart defense. Great defenses put your offense in a better position to score by preventing your opponent from encroaching on your territory. Great defenses put your special teams in the position to make explosive plays by forcing your opponent into difficult late-down scenarios.

In marketing, your best defense is a great brand.

Your brand solidifies your place in the market, and the stronger your brand is in your market, the less ground your competition can gain. The more recognizable your brand is, the easier it is for your sales staff to set up appointments and close deals. The more consumers trust your brand, the more opportunities open up down the road.

Building a strong brand that encapsulates your organizational image and is relatable to your desired market is a tall order. It requires patience, a willingness to adjust, attention to detail, and a big picture vision of what you want your business to convey to consumers.

In the end, though, the best brands, like the best defenses, will put your marketing efforts in the best position to consistently win games.

Committing to the Defense

If you handle your branding right, you'll make the rest of your marketing efforts easy. Skimp, and you'll make every subsequent marketing activity more difficult.

In the digital age, it can be really tempting to hop on a gig-site, like Fiverr, get some cheap logo designs, and close your brand book forever. Resist this urge. Every dollar you save by going with a cheap brand will cost you $100 down the road.

If you have to hire an agency for only one thing, I recommend hiring someone to help you with branding. It's the hardest marketing activity to hire for, and it's the one thing you'll do that should outlive your tenure with the company.

Unless you have the best people in your industry in the following categories, you should probably hire a branding agency:

1. **Market Research:** It's hard to find someone inside your industry that can do objective, hard-hitting market research. It needs to be objective, big picture analysis that doesn't just pertain to what you as a company are looking to accomplish—it needs to encompass everything that could possibly be of use to your business, even it it's information you weren't expecting.

2. **Product Positioning:** Now that you know your market, where do you belong and why? What pain points does your

product or service seek to solve, and what exact words do customers use to express that? Without due diligence in this area, you could spend months, or even years, missing major sales opportunities. Find where you fit into your industry's current landscape, and allow it to inform your brand's messaging.

3. Copywriting: Without great messaging, no one will buy. And I mean no one. Always ensure that the "what" you're communicating to customers is in line with the vision you're trying to sell—in everything from your "About Us" page all the way down to your email campaigns.

4. Design: You don't want an amateur designing your car, or your business' identity. Both will break before you drive them off the lot. Make sure that your logos and imagery convey your brand's message. Your imagery is the first impression people see from you, so spend the resources to make it count.

Playing the Long Game: Branding and Your Web Presence

SEO and branding share a great deal of similarities—not the least of which is that they're both inherently long games. If you focus too heavily on short-term goals with either, you'll be lucky to last six months.

But if you can't expect many short-term results, why are branding and SEO important to your business model?

First and foremost, both branding and SEO are more scalable than traditional business development approaches, which can lead to huge growth down the line. You don't need to train your brand, you just hand it to an agency or your Marketing Director with a budget and watch it grow.

The same is true for SEO—you don't need to let your website "build its territory." Once it owns a keyword, it makes owning the next keyword even easier.

Additionally, both branding and SEO can directly affect your sales if you're willing to wait for them to mature properly. As opposed to hiring a new sales rep, which has a linear growth pattern, effective branding and SEO can often triple or quadruple your sales if you're willing to be patient and invest in the long run.

So, how do branding and SEO work together to accomplish all of this long-term growth?

Climbing the Ranks with Your Brand

Until recently, brand was an afterthought for search engines like Google. For example, you didn't see Pepsi ranking higher than Tab based on brand alone.

For the bulk of the Internet's history, search engine rankings have been a function of the following variables:

- Your site's architecture (how easy it is for Google to read).

- Your site's content (how easy it is for Google to understand what your content is about).

- Your site's popularity (how many other people are

talking about your site).

Traditionally, the third item on this list has been measured by backlinks, but as of 2015, the backlink game has become too easy to manipulate for Google's taste. That's why they've added another major factor to their big three: **searcher activity.**

Searcher activity refers to how users react when they see you on search engines. From a branding perspective, this is huge. Remember all that "user behavior data" we were talking about earlier? Think of this in much the same way.

Google is now using metrics like Search Engine Result Page (SERP), click-through-rate, and bounce rate to determine rankings. If your site is delivering a great user experience that's engaging to users, you're likely to out-rank sites that aren't as well designed or intuitive.

But user experience isn't the only arena where this game is being played. Studies have shown that users are far more likely to click on a Top-Level Domain that they recognize than one that they don't. So, if you're ranking at the same level as one of your competitors, whoever is more recognizable will win out.

This means that your branding efforts offline are now more directly equating to your online popularity, which will in turn equate directly to your rankings. Think about that next time you're at a trade show and see a monster 50' x 50' booth.

Designing an SEO-Style Defense

Now that we've established the importance of branding on your digital presence, how do we build a brand that's going to generate results?

You may be nervous about the prospect of having to compete today with your most visible competitor. The good news is that your only job right now is to assess the playing field and take the next step.

If you're truly dedicated to building a brand for SEO success, here are the tasks you need to accomplish right now:

- Perform a full brand audit to understand who you are

and where you stand in the competitive marketplace.

•   Use Google's Keyword Research Tool to discover what keywords you want to rank for, how frequently they're searched, and how competitive they are.

•   Look at the content on the first page for each of those keywords. What do these pages do well? What do they do poorly? What value do these pages provide the searcher? Then, brainstorm some ways in which you can fill the value gaps you're seeing.

•   Finally, now that you have a general idea of the competitive landscape, it's time to start putting your plan together. Contact a branding or SEO expert and have a conversation about your goals. Walk through your ideas for filling the value gaps to see what else you could be doing. If you truly want to out-rank your competition, you're going to need to find someone who knows how to do that well.

Building a Future-Proof Defense: Branding That Lasts

A lot of great results-driven marketers can make long-term branding blunders because they don't see the value of building a brand that's truly future-proof. Just like your website, however, if you try to shortcut the process now, you're going to pay for it later. And unfortunately, fixing a brand is much harder than fixing a website.

Unlike a website, a brand really isn't *one* thing—it's an amalgamation of all the things that make your company tick.

Every employee, every consumer touch point, every advertisement, every invoice, and every email makes up your brand. In other words, it's not about branding elements like a logo or a color palette, but rather about creating a visual identity, voice, and experience that is authentic to *who you are as a company*.

There are a few core principles of branding that a pretty logo can't fix, and it's your responsibility to do the hard work of establishing a strong foundation for your company's brand. Every future marketing effort will be built upon this foundation, so take it seriously.

Step 1: Start with Self-Reflection

The first step to branding is always self-reflection. What makes you tick? What makes your employees tick? What makes your customers love you? What makes your former customers hate you?

These are your ingredients and they're what you have to work with—branding always starts with the key basics about you as a company. If the inputs you have to work with are "analytic insights" and "creativity," that's great! The output will be top-notch. If your inputs are "cheap" and "efficient," then that's *also* great! Use what you have and who you are to create a brand that reflects both.

Auditing Your Brand Effectively

An effective brand audit is the foundation of your self-reflection. It's not enough to know who you want to be—you need to understand who you already are.

Like it or not, your customers, prospects, and competition already have a perception of your company. As you build your brand, you can choose to talk over their pre-conceived notions, or you can lean into their perceptions and use them to your advantage. In most cases, you're going to be far more successful listening to what the market says about you instead of trying to swim against the current.

By effectively auditing your brand and finding out how it fits into your competitive landscape, you put yourself in the driver's seat when defining your brand's voice and perspective, as opposed to letting others define your narrative.

Here are some easy action items to start with to get your brand audit underway.

- **Google yourself.** See what other people are saying about your brand. What's good? What's bad? Does this match how you see yourself? Why or why not?

- **Google your competitors and ask the same questions.** Is there a void in the marketplace that you can fill?

- **Fill out a full brand audit.** I could spend another 100 pages walking you through the process of doing a complete audit of your brand, but there are far better resources out there to assist in that department. I'd recommend searching for "DIY Brand Audit" to find some comprehensive tools.

Step 2: Create a Brand You Can Live

Now, it's time for everyone's favorite part of branding... actually creating it. Take those elements from Step 1, and think long and hard about how your company can uniquely answer these questions:

- Who do you serve?

- What do you do?

- What is the benefit to your customer?

- What is the key differentiation for your product or service?

These are your four pillars to live by, and they'll create the essence of your company's brand. You'll want to mix all of these elements together to see where you stand against your competition—allow them to inform every aspect of what you look like, sound like, and act like.

If you need help, try simple exercises like word bubbling all of these elements and seeing where there's overlap. You can try the same exercise with your competitors to see what they're emphasizing and, subsequently, what you should avoid.

No matter your approach, you should walk away from this step with a singular identity for your brand.

Use What You Have to Create the Brand You Need

When building a brand, it's important not to be too aspirational. If you want to be a topical, news-worthy brand, but you can't even commit to sending out a few tweets per week, you're setting yourself up to fail.

Take what you learned about your organization during your self-reflection and think about how to tell the most effective story to consumers using the resources you have available.

Here are the main things you'll want to hit:

- **Craft your messaging around the words and phrases your clients use.** Don't try to force the market. Understand where you fit in and double-down on that brand. This is how you can build a brand that feels authentic to everyone involved.

- **Build a visual brand identity system that works for the team you have.** Do you have a ton of designers who lust for raw image files and Illustrator vector art, or do you have design novices at the helm who just need a transparent PNG that they can't screw up? Ask the tough questions about your team and your process when building a visual identity to avoid headache later.

- **Take a deep breath and understand how long branding actually takes.** Building an effective brand, launching it into the marketplace, and gaining traction can take months, even years. If you're doing a DIY branding project, it could take even longer. Be patient and stay the course.

Be Clear About Who You Are (And Who You Aren't)

The biggest mistake that brands make is trying to be too many things to too many people. In order to effectively brand your company, take the results from your brand audit and think about what is actually being said: who do your customers, employees, and the general public think that you are? Are you comfortable being that brand? Why or why not?

Step 3: Find Your Brand Voice

This is the fun part: the practical application. How do you put your brand's essence and voice into action?

Start by taking your brand's identity and crafting it into a personality. Are you approachable, refined, and fun? Are you sophisticated, intellectual, and numerical? Why? Come up with buzzwords that are immediately relatable and recognizable, and that need no further explanation.

Brand voice is an often-overlooked aspect of building an effective brand, but it's one of the most essential elements of a brand that works.

A strong visual identity is nice, but an effective brand voice is what makes your company swift and nimble. Marketing messaging, crisis communication, and sales scripts become exponentially easier when you've already established how your brand is supposed to sound.

Talk to the people who represent your brand

Too often, marketers will hole up in their office for a week and emerge from the ether with a glorious brand document that they mostly made up. That's great for an art project, but if you need something that people can actually use, you should try talking to the people who will use it.

Knowing who will be representing your brand will also help you define how your brand voice will be represented on a larger level. If the purpose of a brand is to help you sell more products, talk to your sales staff about your brand. If you need to communicate your product's superiority, make sure you talk to your product team, etc.

The only way to start building an effective brand is clear, transparent communication with your team. If your brand isn't authentic to your team, it won't be authentic to any-one else.

If you work in a large organization, you'll want to do persona research just like any other marketing activity. Interviewing individuals in the positions you're looking to equip will help you paint a broader picture of your "user base" and will make creating the style guide easier for you down the line.

Ask these individuals about your company, product, and clients. How do they view them? How do their clients view them? What's most important to them?

Here's how to get started:

- **Interview your employees early in the process to get an idea of who they think your brand is.** If you don't think they'll trust you enough to give you honest, candid feedback, bring in a consultant or third-party mediator, or just use tools like SurveyMonkey to collect anonymous responses.

- **The ultimate brand interview checklist:**

- Your top 2-3 salespeople

- 2-3 average salespeople

- Your 2-3 worst salespeople

- Your product development manager(s)

- Your product development team

- Your executive team in a board meeting

- Your executive team one-on-one (you'd be surprised at the difference in answers!)

- Your best (and worst) customers

- **Construct a 2x2 matrix to visualize your marketplace.** Where does your brand currently fit? Where do you want your brand to fit? What will it take to get you from here to there? Can you confidently sell your current position? If so, how do you plan on doing so? This is the foundation of your messaging.

- **Put together some rebranding exercises with your**

team. Take your assessment to the masses and see how they respond. What resonates? What doesn't?

Once you've conducted your interviews, look at the broader picture in context to the way your brand and brand voice will be represented across channels.

Find Your Communication Channels

Next, you'll want to make a list of the places that your brand will be communicated. This includes internal communication and external communication alike.

Look at all of the following questions and make sure you have good answers to each:

- How do we communicate to our team internally? What platforms do we use?

- How do we communicate to our prospects and clients?

- How important is our website? Is it one of our primary tools for educating our clients? If the answer is no, why not?

- What social networks do we use? How do we use them to communicate with our employees, prospects, and customers?

When you're able to answer these questions effectively, you're ready to start the more tangible planning process that will lay the groundwork for your brand's materials and deliverables.

Create an Effective Outline

Start by building a great outline of your brand's voice. You want to make sure that you know when, where, and how your brand's voice will be used at all times. Ideally, it will look something like this:

Our Mission - Why you exist and what purpose you serve?

- What's in your immediate path that you'd like to achieve as a company?

- Who's your target demographic now, and how are you looking to reach them?

Our Vision – Who you want to be when you "grow up?"

- Where do you want to be five years from now? Ten years from now?

- How can you meet the market down the line to attain your "big picture" goals?

Our Brand Voice - A high level overview of what your brand's voice sounds like.

- What do you sound like? What kind of language does your brand use overall?

- What words describe your products, services, and company culture?

Fill in the outline with your brand's unique voice. Make sure that it's authentic to the results of your interviews and not just spin to massage your ego—make this document as genuine as possible.

Once you've filled in the blanks, incorporate this document into your brand identity guidelines and work on enforcing your brand's voice over time.

Your Branding Checklist

If you've completed all these steps, you're well on your way to having an effective, future-proof brand. Now, take all of these ideas and make them into deliverables that you and your team can use easily, and consistently.

Here's a checklist of things you need before you can call it a day:

Visual Assets

- A color palette

- A primary logo and word mark

- A secondary logo mark and/or word mark

- Fonts

- 1-3 preferred textures

- Documented style guide for photography

- Web style guide that dictates website actions (i.e. "A CTA button should do this while in hover state and that while in active state)

- Headshots for employees' social media profiles

- Consistent email signatures

Brand Voice

- A written description of your brand's position in the marketplace.

- A list of your brand's "personality traits" to help your team understand how your brand thinks.

- A documented list of things your brand does and does not say, this includes words you like to use and words you never want to use.

Step 4: Distribute to Every Touch Point

From the Pittsburgh Steelers' "Steel Curtain," to the "Big Blue Wrecking Crew" in New England to your marketing department, great defenses (and brands) are at their best when everyone buys into the same idea—this is how to think about distributing your brand internally.

Map out all of your brand's customer touch points. Whether it's your receptionist answering the phone or an invoice a customer receives, it should look, feel, and sound the same as every other aspect of your brand's personality.

The most effective way to disseminate all of the work you've done on your company's brand is to create the ultimate tool for any marketing department: a style guide.

Your style guide should standardize how you communicate about your company, products, services, and brand. This will typically include things like...

- Guidelines for your brand's appearance, such as restrictions on logo use and color palette options.

- Guidelines for how your brand talks about itself, including details about your brand's voice.

- Guidelines for how you talk about your products,

including technical specifications and legal disclaimers.

Once you've created your style guide, reach out to individuals or their managers and get them a printed copy so that they have these things in their possession at all times. It will be *much* more effective in plain sight than sitting in a shared folder somewhere.

Creating a Style Guide That Won't Be Broken

You've poured countless hours and dollars into building out a killer brand, created your brand style guide, and you're sure that, from here on out, your brand will never be misused again.

Ten minutes after you send out a mass email with your brand guidelines and style guide, however, you see one of your salespeople post your logo on Twitter with a gradient background, *which you clearly forbid.*

This is the bane of every marketer's existence, but it's okay— we've all been there. Because this brand is your baby, it can be easy for you to get upset when someone abuses it, but most of the time they either don't know they did anything wrong or don't know why it's a big deal. Treat every misuse of your brand as a calm, cool, collected adult, and make sure that you always provide concrete guidance on how to use your brand more effectively the next time around.

It begs the question, though, how can you create brand identity guidelines that people won't immediately break?

Build Your Brand Style Guide Around Your "Users"

Remember interviewing your employees and team members in step 3? While that probably helped you develop your brand identity, don't let it be where that information ends.

Because you already have a good idea of who will be using the guide, it will be exponentially easier for you to create a guide that will actually get used. Based on my experience, I'd break your users down into a few categories:

Your Company "Skimmers"

Whether it's young marketers who don't "get" brand identity, executives who don't care about visual consistency, or salespeople who just want their next commission check, these users don't understand why you're sending them a 25-page style guide, so they won't read it. If you call them out on misusing the brand, however, they'll get defensive, and the whole thing will spiral into a larger internal communication issue.

So, how do you get them to pay attention?

Keep it short and sweet. What do they need to know? Are you talking to a salesperson who likes to alter pitch decks? Give them high-level logo requirements (size, proportions, color, and optimal backdrop should suffice), fonts, and a color palate and let them run! What about an executive who has no idea how to properly format his internal memos? Give them letterhead, fonts, and get out of the way.

With this group, it's all about being concise and turnkey in your implementation.

Vocal About Voice

Every marketing department has that one English Lit major who won't shut up about *what the brand is actually trying to say*. This is the formula for great marketing copy, but it can be a pain to build a style guide that they'll approve of. They could care less about how much space you have to put between the logo and the tagline.

Cater to this demographic by creating an effective voice and tone document to complement your visual brand identity. This will help them understand the "why" of your brand so they can keep making magic happen in your copywriting.

Dangerously Detailed Designers

Sometimes, when the game's on the line and the team's down one, a coach just turns to a player wistfully and says, "Go out there and have fun, kid." That's your job with your designers. They want all the details you've been cooking up in that brilliant marketing brain of yours, and this is your chance to give it to them.

Whether your own designers will be using your branding, or designers from other companies incorporating your brand into advertising, these are the type of people who want the 50-page style guide with five pages of logo requirements. If you're catering to this user base, make sure to include *plenty* of details.

Slick Salesmen

So you've got a big sales team that will be using your brand? *Lean into that.* Their top priority is meeting quota, so figure out what words and phrases help them accomplish that goal.

Talk to them about their clients' turn-ons and turn-offs, and ask them for key competitors' slide decks. Find easy wins that can make them look more buttoned up than their competition and they'll love you forever.

Learning from the Spurs: How to Live Your Brand Daily

The San Antonio Spurs are among the most respected franchises in the NBA. They don't play in the biggest market (sorry San Antonio readers), they don't win the championship every year, and they don't have the league's best players from top to bottom.

Still, players flock to this franchise as free agents, making them competitive year in and year out. Why? Coach Gregg

Popovich and the entire front office have developed a consistent team identity and system that they've committed to and won't waiver on.

When the game changes, they adapt, but they don't change who they are at their core—and that's what you should be left with as you finish developing your brand and think about next steps.

This is the hardest part and it takes the longest. If you don't live your brand daily, you don't have a brand to begin with. That's easy to talk about, but what action items can you add to your list **today** that can make this possible...

• Develop a "brand mantra" that you can come back to with regularity. This can be short, long, or in-between, but it should be consistent. If you need a model, look at Google's "What We Believe" page.

• Schedule time in the next 30 days to check in with your team about how they feel they're living the brand. Ask them what they do that's on brand and what they do that strays from that brand. Note, the latter isn't accusatory—

it's just to get candid feedback on the state of your brand.

- Include brand check-ins during regular meetings. If you have a weekly stand-up or daily scrum meeting, add in an item to talk about brand touchpoints. Discuss questions like, "What are you working on?" "What roadblocks do you have?" and "How are you living the brand?" This may seem trite and hokey at first, but if the brand is authentic to your people, it will catch on.

Finally—and this is important—make sure you let it fully bake before you take it out and start playing with it. Far too often, people will look at a brand two weeks after it gets developed and say, "What if we tweaked *this* or changed *that*?" The problem is, the more you allow yourself to tweak, the more it will become your sole solution to every messaging issue moving forward—rendering your brand essentially meaningless.

In these types of instances, *double down* on your brand and dig deeper before abandoning your ideas. Are you having trouble getting your design team to understand the core essence of your brand identity? Sit down with them and ask how you can make it more clear, not how you can change it.

Always remember that brands take time to fully develop, no matter how well you've thought them out—so be patient and ride out the early storm.

Setting Your Formations: the Art of Product Positioning

You've now articulated your company's brand and messaging—but this isn't where your branding efforts end.

No matter how polished your philosophy and no matter how clear your "mantra," a defense is going to function differently depending on where you place your pieces—or which "formation" you line them up in. So, too, it goes with your marketing efforts.

Effective product marketing isn't new, but it's still vital to your success. Your defense will need to continue adjusting to new offensive strategies just like your marketing efforts will continue learning how to properly use new means of communication—but we're still playing the same game.

Whether you're in a product-based organization where every aspect of your product goes through rigorous development and testing, or a service-based organization where your product is more amorphous, the essentials of effective product marketing are the same.

The key is tightening up those essentials to stay malleable and adjust to whatever new is thrown your way.

Unlike tacticians, who often over-rely on phrases like "our product could really be for anyone," great strategists understand...

- What makes their product unique in the marketplace

- Who is a great fit for their product or service, and who should go to a competitor

- What makes that ideal client tick

In this section, we'll walk through each of these ideas and how you can use them to position your product or service in the marketplace. By utilizing your product and brand strengths the right way, you can set yourself up for long-term success by making sure that everything runs effectively, and efficiently.

If you've done product marketing in the past, you've probably heard of the "Seven P's." Let's run through them and talk about how you can get your product up to speed in each.

Product

Let's talk about product specs, the first and most important step of effective product marketing. You need to understand the most up-to-the-minute details of every product or service you're looking to market.

If you're working with software, this mean having a robust understanding of things like API integrations, code base, and technical limitations. If you're working in a service-based organization, like an agency, this could mean having an intimate knowledge of what areas of design your team is most proficient in.

Regardless of the vertical or product type, you can't market what you don't know. Start your process by making a list of every product or service your company offers then list every specification you can think of underneath.

This will include things like…

- **Product features –** e.g. "Removable drill bits, seamless integration with Google Maps, or 24/7 product support."

- **Technical requirements, limitations, and specifications -** e.g. "Leverages a SQL database to collect and analyze information, requires Windows 10 or higher, or not compatible with all mobile devices."

- **Less technical product characteristics –** e.g. "Chewy taffy center, sleek UX, or responsive design."

Don't worry too much about messaging at this stage. Right now, we're just collecting and compiling information for later use.

Price

Next, it's important to understand your pricing structure and how it compares to the rest of your marketplace.

Make a comprehensive list of your competitors, and note their pricing structure for similar products or services. Once you have this information, place it on a spectrum to better understand where you sit competitively. It's important to get a robust understanding of your competition's pricing structure so you can figure out whether you need to adjust your model.

If you're looking for a model to better represent this dynamic, chart out your competition in a 2x2 matrix comparing price and quality. This should give you a great visual to help you understand where your products and services fit into the marketplace.

A note on this: just because your product is the most expensive on the market doesn't mean you need to change. If you're providing a premium service and extraordinary value, you've earned the right to charge a premium for your services. Similarly, if you're a low-cost provider, you need to ensure that your bargain basement prices don't attract the wrong customers, or repel the right ones.

Place

How do you distribute your products? Do you sell directly to your end consumer, or do you have to go through a retailer or distributor? Do you sell primarily online, over the phone, or in-person? For most companies in most industries, the answer will be "a combination" and that's perfectly fine.

This can be the most complicated aspect of product marketing. Even small organizations can have dozens of distribution networks, and you need a high-level understanding of all of them in order to market your products effectively.

To get a good, high-level view of your entire distribution network, begin by making a list of every distribution channel you're leveraging for each product. I prefer to do this via spreadsheet where I can include the following:

- Distribution Channel (online, over the phone, in person, etc.)

- First-Party (I own this channel), Second-Party (A middle-man is exclusively selling my products), or

Third-Party (Distributor or retailer that sells several products like mine)

- Revenue brought in

- Profit margin

- Ongoing costs (Royalties, commission, or anything else that this channel is costing you)

This spreadsheet will give you a great snapshot view of your distribution channels, allowing you to make smarter marketing decisions.

Promotion

When you read the word "promotion" in regards to product marketing, you should think "awareness."

This is a large tent, and you could write an encyclopedia about the tactics behind effective promotion, but for the purposes of this section, let's exclusively focus on promotional channels and brand awareness efforts for your products.

It's important to avoid boxing yourself in when talking about product promotion. Take a moment and write down all of your products or services and make a list of every promotional channel that you're currently leveraging. Next, make a list of all of the channels you'd like to leverage this time next year. Finally, make a list of the channels you would want to leverage if budget wasn't an object.

This will provide you with an accurate snapshot of your product's saturation in the marketplace while providing a roadmap to gain more visibility. It will also let you know how much bandwidth you may have to experiment with new distribution channels, and how many points you can allot to its exploration in a future sprint.

Either way, it's a great opportunity to see what you're doing, what you could be doing, and what you may want to think about scaling back on, as is consistent with on up-to-the-minute industry information.

Process

How do your customers make their decisions? In the B2B world, this can be an extremely important and often ignored question.

Usually, the answer will be found by talking to your sales staff. If you don't understand your ideal market's usual buying cycle, it's your responsibility to identify common stumbling blocks, barriers to entry, and objections before they occur.

Sit down with your sales staff and ask them things like...

- How many conversations do you usually have to have before someone makes a decision?

- What key stakeholders are usually involved in a purchase?

- Does the decision happen over minutes, hours, days, weeks, or months? Why?

- What incentive does the customer have not to buy? How constrained is their budget, and what limits or red tape does our ideal client have standing in their way from purchasing?

We'll talk more directly about sales support a bit later, but this will help you map out your sales cycle more accurately. Once you understand this information, you'll be able to take it into consideration when thinking about any changes, adjustments, and future promotional opportunities that the market deems necessary.

People

As a strategic marketer, you need to have a robust understanding of what your human capital looks like.

If you're working for a large organization, you may have a team of 30 people plus a bevy of agencies. If you're working for a small organization, you may be a department of one. You can only market with the resources you have.

The easiest way to visualize this is by hours. If your department is comprised of you, plus four employees, you have five people times 40 hours, or 200 man hours a week.

Earlier in this book, I discussed how agile marketing could help quantify these hours into a manageable series of "points" but in order to future-proof your marketing department, you can't bite off more than you can chew. This will lead to burnout among your staff, in-fighting, tension, and, ultimately, employee turnover.

Focus on doing a manageable amount of work *really, really* well, not attempting to do everything just for the sake of trying to keep up.

Physical Environment

Finally, we need to take into consideration the physical environment where this product will be bought. For retailers, this means thinking about the in-store experience. For an eCommerce company, this means having a robust understanding of your website's user experience.

Understanding your physical environment will put you in the consumer's shoes, allowing you to make more informed decisions on how best to improve their experience while keeping with what makes you, *you.*

Don't forget that the more you understand about your customer's experience, what they enjoy about your product, and your overall brand recognition, the better your big picture vision will be.

Recap: Leaning on Your Defense

In 2000, the Baltimore Ravens won the Super Bowl despite having, statistically, one of the poorer offenses in the league. How did they do it? With one of football's all time best defenses.

A great brand, like a great defense, lifts your entire team up. It's not the only piece of the puzzle, and a great brand won't solve all of your marketing woes, but it doesn't matter how good your offense is if you can't at least stop your opponent every once in awhile.

Likewise, you can sell to everyone in your target market, but if your brand doesn't own any territory in that space, they'll all switch to your competitors. We start here so we can establish our territory before we try to put points on the board.

The key is making sure that, as you expand your efforts into lead generation and sales support, you don't forget the central identity your brand expresses. Whenever you hit a snag or a bump in the road, don't panic—just go back to the essentials of your brand's foundation for the answer.

Play Calls - Defense

Here's a list of things you can do today to develop and improve your defense.

○ Perform an audit of your current brand, as well as your three biggest competitors.

○ Identify and document your brand's voice.

○ Create a formalized visual identity for your brand.

○ Identify your product or service's position in the marketplace, including your competitive advantages and key barriers to purchase.

Putting Points on the Board: Using Diversified Lead Generation to Create Offense—and Revenue

Let's stick with the football metaphor for a moment.

In football, an offensive strategy generally takes a two-pronged approach: your running game and your passing game.

Your running game refers to your ability to hand the ball off to your running back, allowing blockers to open up holes for what often amounts to small gains. Occasionally, a running back breaks free for *huge* sprints across the field, but generally speaking, these types of plays only result in your offense getting three to five yards at a time.

The real key to the running game is the way it opens up your passing game. By forcing the defense to stay in tight to defend against the run, an offense opens up the opportunity to beat them down field with a pass, which has the potential to go for many more yards.

This is the best way to think about your content and lead generation—a balanced game of small, intermittent gains that can open up larger opportunities down the line. Too much emphasis on huge risks downfield, and the defense can just sit back and knock everything down. Too much dependence on the short gains, however, and you'll have difficulty outpacing your competition.

In this section, we're going to focus on how to create a balanced offensive attack. We'll start with a solid ground game and then, once we force our opponents to defend against that, we'll be able to start attacking through the air. Finally, we'll discuss traditional lead generation channels and why the Statue of Liberty play has given us some of the greatest moments in football history.

The Run Game: Creating Consistently Great Content

I regularly talk to tacticians who are passionate about creating world-class content. This is a great, ambitious goal, and I admire them for it.

Here's the truth about content, however: for most marketers, you don't need world-class content.

That's not to say you shouldn't have high standards. You should have very high standards for every piece of content you create. But if your game plan is to exclusively produce world-class content and hope that it leads to more traffic, you better have a few million in the bank dedicated to your content creation.

What strategists understand is that you really just need *good-enough* content at a world-class scale. Instead of focusing on each blog being a masterpiece, your focus should be on making each blog solve a problem, answer a question, and provide value.

Your running game content should include your blogs, email strategy, and social media campaigns—each of which are small, incremental tasks that over time can build you a sustainable, reliable, and trusted online brand that's sure to open up your bigger plays.

In this section, it's key to remember not to fuss over the details—just crank out valuable content at a regular frequency. You can always optimize around the margins once you have a system in place.

Blogging at a World-Class Scale

So what does "world-class scale" really mean? In an environment where most businesses are lucky if they produce content on a weekly basis, I believe that consistency and volume are the elixirs for success.

Businesses that produce content at a world-class scale typically do three things extraordinarily well:

- **They're consistent.** If they blog on Monday and Thursday, there's a new post up every single Monday and Thursday, with no interruptions, at the exact same time.

This is good for the business, good for users, and good for Google.

- **They're scheduled.** The best content-engines schedule content at least two weeks in advance. They're never under the gun.

- **They're nimble.** The best content producers keep their schedule loose so that they can pivot when the market calls for it.

Personally, I recommend that every business aspiring to produce content should blog at least twice a week. This gives you over 100 chances a year to get it right, and this is the kind of scale that allows real opportunities to open up. Just like running the football, there will be plenty of short gains, but every once in awhile, you could open up the right hole and see something take off.

At the end of the day, the most successful content producers aren't the ones that produce the highest-quality content—they're the ones that produce content with the highest consistency.

Worth noting, though: your content should never, ever sacrifice user experience just for the sake of getting it out the door. Remember, the future of your online presence is in the way users interact with your site, so don't let your content schedule get in the way of the whole point of creating content in the first place.

You can have all the consistency and preparation in your content you want, but if, at the end of the day, you don't provide value to your reader, they'll just ignore your content on a weekly basis.

To simplify everything a bit, take a look below. **If your content can satisfy these two checklists, then it's good-enough content:**

SEO Checklist

[Should check at least ⅔ of these boxes]

- Is my target keyword in my title?

- Is my target keyword in at least one H2 tag?

- Is my target keyword in the body of the post?

- Is my target keyword used as alt-text for a blog image?

- Is my target keyword used in stylized text, such as bold or italics?

- Do I include variations of my target keyword throughout the piece?

- Does my post link to at least one other post on my website?

Effective Content Checklist

[Should check at least one]

- Does it provide demonstrable value?

- Does it answer a common industry question?

- Does it provide readers with a sense of identity?

- Does it give readers an "emotional gift?"

- Does it reinforce readers' worldview?

Getting Spam Out of the Game: Future-Proof Email Strategy

I will bet my career on this sentence: Email isn't going anywhere.

Bad email marketers will argue that email is dead. *"Younger users don't use email,"* they'll say. *"They use social media to communicate. Therefore email is dead."*

Well, if you're trying to sell Mountain Dew, that might be accurate, but if you're trying to sell literally anything else, email is an invaluable channel that you have to get right if you want your digital efforts to scale effectively.

Email marketing has a few unique advantages that make it my vehicle of choice to build marketing efforts on:

- **Email is (virtually) free to send. -** If you build a healthy email list, you can market to them once a month or once an hour and it costs you the same amount.

- **Email can be as intimate as you want. -** An advertisement doesn't let you talk to a real person, but your email efforts can look and feel like a one-to-one interaction.

- **Email converts.** - Period. For most products and industries, it's the channel that's closest to a purchase decision.

- **Email can feed every other channel.** - If you want to run a Facebook campaign, you can leverage your email list to target users that are exactly like the users that have already bought from you in the past.

Unfortunately for marketers (but fortunately for users), Gmail has been aggressively working to keep promotional emails out of the inbox. The spam filter has a new partner, the Promotions Tab, and these same principles will be applied to other inboxes soon.

So, in the ever-changing landscape of email platforms, how can you build an email strategy that is truly future-proof? It comes down to two main components: formatting and user behavior data.

Formatting Emails to Make People (And Gmail) Happy

Gmail wants users to get emails that they like, and not get emails they don't like.

What emails do you like? Probably emails from your friends. Maybe emails from your coworkers. Heck, you probably really look forward to getting an email from your grandma.

So let me ask you this: when's the last time you built a complex, HTML template to send an email to your grandma?

Email platforms are smarter than ever and they're using those smarts to weed out marketers. That's not to say that there's no place for fully-designed and developed emails, but that place is pretty limited.

The most effective emails are the ones that get seen, and the ones that get seen are generally the lightest. The more code you have to write, the more buttons you have, the more you have to worry about how things will render in different browsers, the less effective your email will be.

Unfortunately, most marketers don't think that far in advance when their design agency is building them an email template. They get really excited about rich features and imagery, without realizing the implications of these design choices.

Here's what I recommend to organizations that want to build a truly future-proof email template:

- Create a standard template that is both on-brand and extremely close to a basic plain-text design. You can always add in-line imagery if you choose, but work to keep this template extremely simple. This is your future-proof template. It should look good, but the code base should be extremely light.

- Create a slightly more upscale template for special uses. This can have a header image, some image-rich content blocks, etc. This is a sometimes snack—a little running play that you hope goes for big yardage, but one that you don't run often enough to become habit—perhaps once a quarter or so. Don't send this template out for ongoing email marketing, but it can be really helpful for things like event emails or big brand pivot emails.

- Finally, you can create heavier templates that are campaign-specific if you so choose. If you want to run a campaign with a dense, heavy email template, that's fine, but it should be the exception, not the rule. Think of this like running a double-reverse lateral in football—a crazy trick-run play you may see once every three games. Run these types of plays once in awhile and you may be able to break through for big gains. Run it too often, though, and it loses its punch and becomes predictable and gimmicky.

Your Quarterback Sneak: How to Increase Your Email Conversion Rates Without Pissing Anyone Off

Okay. So now that we've created a template that will help your email get seen, how do we get people on your email list? More importantly, how do you build your email list without pissing off your subscribers? We've all been on the other end of a spammy relationship, and no one wants to re-create that.

The best thing you can do here is to provide really high-quality, downloadable content. The process is simple:

- Provide a form at the bottom of every blog post you

write offering premium content.

• Keep the blog post and the premium content tangentially related. You don't want to offer "The Ultimate Guide to Steak" to users that are reading a blog on "12 Easy Vegan Recipes."

• When users fill out the form, email them the content. Don't allow it to download directly on your page. You want to train them that when you email them, they receive good content.

• Finally, program your email automation to ask for an opt-in. This is the most important aspect of your email marketing efforts. It's important to get it right. This shows your users that you respect them and starts the relationship on the right foot.

Making a Great First Impression with Your Email Automation

You never get a second chance to make a first impression, and once a user is trained to do something with your emails, it's hard to un-train them.

If users routinely open your emails and click through the links, they will continue to do so until you send them content that they don't like. If users routinely delete your emails, they will continue to do so, no matter how interesting your content may be.

That's why it's paramount to capitalize on your email introduction sequence. This is the first time that a user is welcoming you into their home. It's your responsibility to treat them with respect. Here are some ways that you can optimize your welcome sequence for better list health:

- **Use preview text to your advantage.** Hard-code in preview text that tempts users to open. My favorite trick? End your preview text with an ellipses. It makes your users beg for...

- **Double opt-in.** You already sent them one email with a piece of great content. That's fantastic. Next, send them an email introducing yourself and ask them to double opt-in. Users love this transparency and respect.

- **If they don't opt-in, give them a few chances.** Don't be afraid to send a "last chance" email. These tend to convert well.

- **Build an automation sequence that is custom-tailored to that interest.** Based on the content they downloaded, you probably know what they're looking for in their content, so use that information to help inform how you interact with them.

- **End every email asking for a reply**. Ask a question and then, use these exact words. "Hit reply and let me know! I read every response."

Beating the Slump: How to Come Up with Great Email Content Every Week

Email automation is easier than people make it out to be. You dedicate one week to building a great drip campaign and then it runs automatically for years, bringing in leads.

Generating consistent, ongoing email content, however, can be extremely difficult.

Let's say your welcome sequence lasts 8 weeks. What do you

send those users who are done with the welcome sequence? You can't just keep running the same play over and over again or you'll become predictable and lose value to your audience. You have to keep the momentum up, lest your users forget about you.

This is where ongoing email marketing can get difficult. *How do you come up with consistently great email content every week?*

First, commit to a pace. It's okay to send an email once a month, but keep it consistent. Once you have your pace, you can create a content calendar. Starting out, I advise that clients keep this extremely high level.

For example, in November, you're going to talk about family. That's a broad topic for a broad month. You can write one email or five. Just commit yourself to a theme and a cadence.

Perhaps most importantly, though, always make sure to be personal, honest, timely, and flexible in your content.

Let's break each of those down individually:

- **Personal** - Don't be afraid to be vulnerable. Show sides of your personality and brand that you may not normally show. This is an exclusive list, so treat it as such and talk to your audience like close friends.

- **Honest** - Don't posture or try to put on a show. Be honest about what you know and what you don't. It's okay for your brand to be naive in certain areas.

- **Timely** - When big shakeups happen in your industry, your customers look to you for guidance. Be there to provide it. If you're an expert in real estate and the housing crisis hits, you need to be willing to get an email out stat to help your list understand what's going on.

- **Flexible** - You're driving into work when, all of sudden, you're struck with inspiration. Ride that wave. It doesn't matter that you have something else scheduled for today. Reschedule it for next week. Always be open for inspiration to strike.

In the end, your email marketing campaign is all about treating your customer like a person, not a piece of market potential. Never forget that your users are opening your email for pleasure, not business, so remember the golden rule: market unto others as you would have them market unto you.

Data Hygiene and You: How Poor List Management Takes Points Off The Board

The final piece of the email puzzle is your data hygiene.

Remember earlier when we talked about the importance of user behavior data? Gmail remembers. In fact, Gmail remembers a lot of things about your users and how they interact with your marketing.

It uses this data to filter users' inboxes, so if your email list has a high unsubscribe or spam report rate, Gmail is going to filter out all of your messages, even for people who usually open your emails. If that sounds scary, it should—but the good news is that you can prevent it from happening by proactively monitoring your user behavior data.

For example, let's take three commonly-used KPIs (Key Performance Indicators) for email marketing: open rate, click-through rate, and unsubscribe rate. Let's just say that, on average, your industry sees a 25% open rate, 5% click-through rate, and 1% unsubscribe rate. If you sent to everyone on your list 100% of the time, then you would see these exact same numbers.

Fortunately, we can isolate the population down to your best subscribers. Let's say we only want to send to anyone who has opened your last three emails. Now, you're only sending to ⅓ of the population, but your open rate skyrockets. So does your click through rate, and no one unsubscribes or reports the email as spam.

Now, let's say you do this once a week. You only send to your absolute best, most engaged subscribers. Your list health and sender score are off the charts, so when you decide to send an email to your full list, Gmail delivers far more of these emails to primary inboxes than any of your competitors.

This is the methodology that can not only keep your email list healthy, but can also keep your sender score high enough that every email you send will have a meaningful impact on your list.

But if you don't send to everyone all the time, aren't you missing out on sales?

No, you're not. You're systematically weeding out people who are less engaged and less responsive. They are telling you something with their actions, and it's your responsibility as a marketer to listen. Instead of hitting them week after week with messages, you should focus on sending them only your best messages.

One of the reasons that it's tough to talk about list hygiene is because you don't typically see the losses it creates. These losses aren't massive and they're usually not immediate, but they're the product of small, consistent mistakes that could have helped you make a sale in an alternate universe. It's the equivalent of marching all the way to the red zone and then kicking a field goal instead of scoring a touchdown. You may deem it a success because you walked away with points, but you're also leaving points on the field.

Don't let this happen to you. An unengaged prospect will remain unengaged unless acted upon by an engaging force.

Be that engaging force.

Dividing Your Data: How to Engage Through
Behavior Segmentation

Let's imagine three buckets. Let's say bucket one is "High Engagement," two is "Medium," and three is "Low."

Those high engagement prospects are going to like just about anything you say. You could send them a series of drunk texts at two in the morning and they'd probably respond (please don't do that). Instead, feel free to shoot them more frequent, informal emails. These could range from thought leadership all the way down to your thoughts on something in pop culture.

Your medium bucket might like you, but they don't really care about you. They're not looking to unsubscribe, but they're not looking to hear your thoughts on the new Avengers movie, either. Send them your best-testing emails from your "highly engaged" bucket. This will help you better understand what resonates with your marginal consumer.

Finally, that low engagement bucket barely cares enough

to stay on your list. They should only be receiving things like discount codes or aggressive branding campaigns.

This is a simple but powerful way for you to segment your list and maximize engagement.

Applying the Timeless Principles to Social Media

This may seem like pretty late in the game to start talking about social media. We've made it nearly halfway through a book that's mostly about digital marketing and I'm just now mentioning social media?

Am I crazy... or just pragmatic?

The key thing to remember about social media as it relates to your content is that you don't own it. Your Facebook audience could go away tomorrow if Zuckerberg decided it was a good idea, and if you think that sounds crazy, you're forgetting the EdgeRank controversy and how much more difficult it's become for businesses to be seen on social media since 2010.

That being said, for a lot of businesses, social media is still an invaluable tool. I'll even break down the B2C stereotype and say that it can be just as invaluable for B2B companies. The problem is that there's no one-size-fits-all solution for social media, but no one wants to tell you that, because they want you to believe that they have the "9 Instagram Hacks That GUARANTEE *Blah Blah Blah*."

If you're *really* interested in doing the work to make social media a strong portion of your marketing's running game, it's important to focus on where your target market is, what they want while they're there, and how you're uniquely positioned to provide that service consistently over time.

Where Your Target Market Is

This is the first and most important step of any social media strategy. There are almost no universal truths in social media marketing, because there are almost no universal truths in human nature. You should build a Facebook Page and a Google My Business Page just to help users find you, but after that, you need to stop and take inventory of where your market actually lives online.

This can be done with Experian data, focus groups, online surveys, or even just some simple Googling. How you acquire this information is going to be mostly determined by your budget and timeline, so I'll let you figure out what fishing pole you want.

Meanwhile, here are some of the answers I hear routinely from clients, to give you an idea of where the industry sits currently...

- "My clients aren't online. They tend to be older professionals that only use Facebook to catch up with their family." (Notice the contradiction? I hear that once a month.)

- "My ideal customer is younger. They're on Instagram and Snapchat. Most of their online life happens on their phone."

- "I'm trying to target professionals looking for a career change, and they use LinkedIn to network."

If you really want to build a resilient social media strategy that can generate results, you need to be thinking like our second and third example combined—don't be naive and don't guess.

You should know, on average, what social networks your target audience tends to use, what devices they access those networks from, and even what *browsers* they use. This will help you deliver a world-class social media presence.

What They Want

Next, you need to focus on what your audience is looking for on social media. For 0/10 of them, the answer will be your product or service, and that's okay! You just need to be self-aware. That's the first step.

Usually, the answer is some level of social validation. From political rants on Facebook, to live-Tweeting events, to posting new career accomplishments on LinkedIn, no one is on social media to yell into a void. They're there for the social interaction—engaging with their network and receiving a substantiation of their worldview.

So, that being said, what kind of social validation does your target market want from social media? Do they want their friends to think they're cool? Do they want their boss to think they're smart? Do they want their in-laws to think they're a stand-up guy?

Write these social validations down and make them your go-to whenever you're wondering what to post or share. Before you hit the "send" button on any tweet, ask yourself, "How will this make my followers feel better about themselves?"

What You've Got

Now, the rubber hits the road. It's time for you to provide that social validation to your audience.

Take a look at your brand, product, and service. What is it about your company that can make your ideal prospect look smart to their boss? Probably quick statistics, bite-sized quotes, or shareable articles that reinforce how thoughtful that employee is, right?

What about your company could make a college kid look cool? Maybe an air of exclusivity? Maybe a specific Snapchat filter they can only unlock in a certain area of your store.

Maybe you have a contest on Instagram where the five best photos featuring your product will be put on a billboard in Times Square.

Hopefully you're starting to understand why there is no "one-size-fits-all" solution for social media. It can be wildly effective for most companies, but the wildly effective solution for B2B software is going to be dramatically different than the winning idea for a pizza chain down the street.

One core truth remains the same, however: people go to social media for validation. The good news is that no matter who you are, you can provide that validation to them in one way or another.

Recap: Making the Run Game Count

I get it—the world of patient content creation, email templates and list segmentation, with a splash-less social media campaign certainly isn't the sexiest part of your marketing strategy. But it's a vital part nonetheless.

The run game isn't pretty, and just like an offensive line

pushes forward to help its running back gain *every inch*, so too will every piece of content you create help you inch forward in your brand perception and audience base.

Of course, every so often, your content will break free in the open field and score some series points. A blog may get picked up by a major outlet, a social media post may go viral, or maybe an email converts an unusually high volume of sales—but that's not what we're trying to accomplish here. This is all about creating small, predictable gains that can open up your passing game to go long.

Airing It Out: Generating a High-Octane Offense

Alright, folks. This is the show we've all been waiting for, the final piece of your lead generation strategy: the passing game.

In the last section, we talked about your running game—building a consistent, reliable stream of web traffic that you can convert consistently into revenue. Now, it's time to talk about the plays that make SportsCenter. Paid ads, trade shows, and bringing in leads en masse.

Lead generation is the star quarterback, the homecoming king, the town hero who throws the perfect pass as time expires to win the big game against Rival Prep Academy.

It's not so much that this is the *most* important part of your marketing strategy, but it's the most visible, and has the most direct revenue correlation. Thus, it's the thing that many marketers tend to focus on first and foremost.

It comes down to this: while branding and positioning are essential, lead generation is what will land you a quarterly bonus.

So let's talk about it.

Don't Forget Who You Are: Balancing Brand with Sales Strategy

We'll begin by talking at a high level about the institutional savvy necessary to balance your brand in a sales-driven organization. If you've ever worked for a numbers-oriented boss, you know how tough this can be. It's like that star quarterback being drafted by the pros and becoming a huge NFL star while trying not to forget all their friends back in Hometown, USA.

Doing what's right for your brand in the long run will often come at the expense of today's numbers, and today's numbers are often what dictates whether you get a promotion or a pink slip.

How do you strike the balance?

Remember earlier when I said that all marketing can be broken down into branding, lead generation, and sales support? Similarly, within lead generation every activity can be broken down into one of two requests:

- Bring us more leads.

- Bring us better leads.

Marketing departments should allocate efforts to both sides of the spectrum, but your mindset when working on lead generation efforts should always be, "Will this bring in more leads, better leads, or both?"

Now, let's break those down individually.

Request 1: Bring Us More Leads

This is the most common request you'll get from your sales team. They want to throw the ball more, because the more they throw, the better the chances are that they'll hit their quota.

When looking to build out this side of the spectrum, look for channels that offer an immediate return and rank them based on the following criteria:

- How expensive are they?

- How much return do you expect from them?

- How quickly do you expect to see that return?

Ideal channels for this side of the spectrum have low fixed and upfront costs with high variable costs. They usually include a strong call to action, incentivize quick decision-making, and will deliver more leads at a lower cost, putting your sales process in the driver's seat.

Common channels might include...

- Facebook advertising

- Direct mail (we'll talk more about the value of direct mail in a digital world later)

- Google AdWords

Common Pitfalls

When you're heavily focused on quick returns and increasing today's top-line revenue, there are some common pitfalls that can drive a wedge between sales and marketing.

In order to preserve this vital relationship, it's paramount that you do everything you can to avoid making these mistakes:

- **Over-Reliance on One Channel:** I've seen it dozens of times. You get in a rhythm on one channel, they change the rules, and the leads dry up. Treat your marketing efforts like your 401k—*diversification is king.*

- **Black or Grey-Hat Tactics:** If you have to ask if it's legitimate, don't do it. Period. If it sounds too good to be true, it will get your website banned from the Internet. There are no shortcuts in future-proofing.

- **Breaking the Golden Rule:** Remember our golden rule: market unto others as you would have them market unto you. If you're buying lists and emailing them without warning, don't be surprised when you get a scarlet "S" for Spammer.

- **Lack of Sales Support:** We'll talk more about sales support in the next section, but suffice it to say that it doesn't matter how many leads you're sending—if you're not supporting your sales staff so that they can effectively close them, you're not doing your job.

Request 2: Bring Us Better Leads

After you start bringing consistent leads to your sales staff, they'll inevitably ask for better leads.

This is a common request for a reason—salespeople don't want to weed through hundreds of executives to find the one with a budget to buy. They want to focus their efforts on accounts they can win, and it's your job to facilitate that desire.

When looking to build out this side of the circle, you should prioritize channels and tactics based on the following criteria:

- What's the average lifetime value of a single "won" deal?

- How many deals would this channel allow you to win?

- Will this channel bring you leads on a recurring basis?

You'll notice that I didn't include price here, and that's

intentional. While you'll definitely have budget constraints that force different avenues to compete for your marketing resources, this side of the circle is about value received, not bargain hunting.

If you need to make more happen with less, it's better to offload some of the work onto your Business Development Representative. They're paid to prospect and can shoulder some of the burden. When your focus shifts to delivering high-quality leads, however, it's up to you to shoulder the burden of prospecting, and that will require much less price sensitivity.

Some common channels for this side of the circle include:

- Tradeshows

- Bottom-Funnel Inbound marketing

- Thought leadership

Common Pitfalls

Even though this is usually thought of as the more "reputable" side of the lead gen circle, it still has plenty of common traps that marketers fall into on a regular basis:

- **Getting Too Price Sensitive:** You get what you pay for, and it's hard to bargain shop on this side of the spectrum. If you're going to get gun shy when the bill comes, focus on quantity over quality.

- **Not Taking Creative Risks:** If you're not willing to take some chances, it doesn't matter how much you spend on content, which news outlets cover your product launch, or how big your tradeshow booth is. You have to stand out to land the business.

- **Expecting Immediate Return:** This is the patience side of the circle. If you want better leads, they'll take a while. Be patient and always give it at least six months.

The Option Run: Third Party Content Distribution

Once you've established a solid content running game, you can use it to your advantage by moving to the outside and trying to expand your field to different sites and platforms. This type of lead generation can exponentially help raise your brand awareness, and can give you great, new leads from people looking to buy your services or products.

Third parties simply refer to platforms that you don't own, but that allow you to post or upload single pieces of content to reach a wider audience.

This includes...

- Third-party media, such as bylines, guest blogs, or press coverage

- Video hosting platforms like YouTube and Vimeo

- Content-hosting platforms like Medium

It should be noted that this is all organic, not paid. We don't lump in things like paid social advertisements or YouTube pre-roll ads here. The key to establishing a great third party content strategy is rooted in solid brand messaging and effectively vetting the million options at your disposal when it comes to third-party channels.

You may be asking yourselves why we included social media in the previous section, and not this one, despite it being a platform you don't technically "own."

As you've already seen, social media is a little different. It involves a consistent effort over time and thus should be one of the foundational elements of your digital marketing strategy. A great social media strategy, however, will certainly improve your third party content, be it more views for a YouTube video that you share with your audience, or a guest blog opportunity you're offered based on your existing online audience.

Picking Your Play: Determining Your Unique Take for Third Parties

Let's start by talking about third-party media. This includes guest bylines for your local newspaper, guest blogs for industry publications, and featured posts on other third-party platforms. *The biggest mistake that people make with third-party opportunities is not carving their own unique take.*

When writing for these outlets, you have two obligations, in this order:

- **To the reader -** Make a conscious effort to understand your reader's perspective on this platform. Who is this website's typical reader? What do they like? What do they dislike? The better you write for their audience, the more likely they'll ask you back.

- **To your company –** You're there to spread a message. That message should be clear, concise, and to the point. It should be consistent throughout the piece, and should be consistent with the other third-party media you're releasing.

Everything you write for third-parties should stay on message. You don't want to do an op-ed talking about the changing pace of technology one day and then write a guest blog about the "good ol' days" of analog the next.

Instead, you should have one cohesive message that transcends audience or channel.

For example, let's say that your overall message this quarter is, "Our new product is revolutionizing the way people brush their teeth." That could take a lot of different forms for different outlets...

- In Fast Company, your op-ed could be about how your founder identified the toothbrush industry as ripe for disruption.

- In Mashable, your guest post could be about this tooth-brush's awesome new features and how it's revolutionizing personal care products.

- In your local newspaper, it could be about the culture behind this innovation—how your employees worked together to identify the need for a new toothbrush.

- In Dental Care Monthly, it could be about the health benefits of this new toothbrush technology and its impact on the dentist community.

Notice that all four of those articles are dramatically different, but they're all preaching the exact same message.

It's paramount that you find a unique take for every publisher you work with. This will help you resonate effectively with their audience and generate more buzz around each piece.

How to Find (And Get) The Right Third-Party Opportunities

Outside of hiring a full Public Relations agency, it can be really difficult to find guest blogging opportunities that you can land. Editors and reporters generally rely on their relationships to fill guest slots, and establishing the right relationships within your industries can take years.

So how do you get these bylines?

To start off, it's important to understand that no one really cares about your brand. The good news, though, is that you don't need to land a Forbes byline today.

Instead, focus on working your way up through the ranks of local niche blogs. This allows you to build a solid backlink pro-file, a decent following, and establish a Rolodex of industry connections that could provide access to gatekeepers at the next level.

I always start with a Google search and an Excel spreadsheet. Search for as many industry-related blogs as you can find. Try to find at least 25, get the basic contact information, and take close notes on their audience—who are they? What are their demographics? What are their interests? What type of language do they use?

Take this information and put it in a table for easy access.

Vetting Third Parties for Sustainability

Since you'll be doing a lot of work with smaller, niche sites, it's important to consider the fact that not everyone is as smart as you. In a perfect world, everyone you work with would have bought this book, so they would all know how to prevent their website from getting penalized by Google.

Unfortunately, though, my book sales aren't nearly high enough for that to be the case.

Let's say The Simple Tooth wants to increase their search traffic, and because Dr. Timmy has never read my book, he's hired a seedy SEO company with a history of getting websites blacklisted by Google. All of a sudden, that backlink from The

Simple Tooth goes from an asset to a liability.

Now, of course you've prepared for this with your backlink audits (which we'll learn about in part 3 of this book), but how can you prevent this to begin with?

Moz has a tool called the "Open Site Explorer" that allows you to analyze the backlink profile of any website—including your competition, your clients, and even third-party blogs. Check the backlinks on any website you guest post on to see things like...

- **Domain Authority -** Is this website considered authoritative or not? In other words, is it respected in the industry? Is it more authoritative or less authoritative than mine? (Note - I like to use Alexa.com to assess a site's authority, but other useful tools include Moz or SERPWoo.)

- **Spam Score -** You don't want to have to disavow this link later, especially if you spend hours writing and editing a byline. Get ahead of it by seeing if their backlink profile raises any red flags before you do the work.

- **Who is linking to them? -** You're likely to get linked to by the same people who link to this site. If The Moldy Molar has bad backlink practices, and they like to link to The Simple Tooth, that could be a bad omen.

Making the Connection with Your Third Party Sites

Once you've filled out the table, reach out to your contact and *make each outreach message personal*. Don't blanket spam them. Tell them what you like about their blog and ask them what their policy is on guest blogging.

For example, you may want to say…

Dear Dr. Timmy,

Hope all is well! I work for Denta.ly, a startup in the toothbrush space. I've been reading your blog, The Simple Tooth, for months and I really like it. I especially like the conversational tone of your articles. I wanted to drop you a note to see what your policy on guest blogging is. There are a few articles I'm working on that your readers might enjoy, including:

- *3 Reasons Your Old Toothbrush Costs You Money*

- *Top 10 Electric Toothbrush Alternatives*

- *The Ultimate Guide to Picking an Electric Toothbrush*

Thanks for your consideration! I'll reach back out in a week to see where you're at.

Thanks!

Kevin

Make sure to continually follow-up. As someone who's been on the other side of this request, I can easily ignore one email, but three replies over three weeks forces my hand. Don't be pushy, but make sure your message gets through. Remember, content sites are looking for content to publish, but standing out in their inbox is how you get results.

Once you've built a network of niche blogs that you've been featured on, you have a much more compelling pitch to more mid-level third parties.

For example, six months down the road, it would be really easy for Kevin to take his byline in The Simple Tooth, email it to Fast Company and see if they'd be interested in publishing a future guest blog. You're still not guaranteed anything, but this strategy substantially increases your credibility.

The Shotgun Formation: Why We Focus on Paid Ads Last

The last piece of your passing game consists of everything that you pay for. We're talking paid ads, sponsored posts, "Advertorials" and the like.

Think of this piece as your shotgun formation—which refers to an offensive system in football that emphasizes deep passes down the field and huge gains all at once. While this sounds like a no-brainer kind of system that should be used whenever possible, the shotgun formation, like paid ads, is only successful if the rest of the team is firing on all cylinders.

A team that can't effectively run, block, and complete short passes has no business with the shotgun formation, and the same goes for paid ads. Without a strong foundation in your marketing strategy, paid ads are just long, incomplete throws downfield.

There are several reasons this is the case, including:

- **Funnel optimization:** You don't want to pour a bunch of money into ads until you've perfected the process of converting that traffic into revenue.

- **Escalating costs with diminishing benefits:** Paid ads will almost universally go up in cost, and down in efficacy. It's best to use them as a supplementary resource.

- **It doesn't generate an asset:** Paid ads can be effective ways to drive traffic and revenue, but they don't generate long-term assets, such as a webpage that drives organic traffic or a highly responsive email list.

- **It can be taken away at any time:** If your plan A is something that you can get banned from, it's a bad plan A. These channels are the most susceptible to changes in technology and the marketplace, so if they're your first line of defense, you're extremely vulnerable. I've seen people have advertising rights revoked from paid channels, and believe me—it can set your marketing strategy back significantly if you've placed too much into it.

If you're anything like a lot of clients I've worked with in the past, at some point you've probably dealt with pressure to deliver results *immediately*. Paid ads can be great for this, but they're not conducive to building a future-proof marketing strategy.

Once you've established a solid foundation and built upon that foundation with effective third-party growth, you're ready to start tackling paid channels.

How to Know If Paid Channels Are Right for You

All this being said, how do you know if you're ready to invest in paid ads?

I don't believe that paid channels are right for everyone. For most businesses, a solid digital presence plus maybe a few direct mail pieces could deliver them more business than they know what to do with. That said, it's hard to know when you're in the middle of building your marketing strategy whether that describes your business or not.

Ultimately, even if you're ready to accept all of the risks listed above, as a marketing asset paid ads are still a risk.

First off, they're expensive. Second, they're pay-to-play. This means that you'll continually need to pump money in if you want to get anything back out. If you can put an equal amount of energy into two things, and one gives you an asset and the other doesn't without a significant amount of money, then I will almost always advise that you focus on the former.

Most importantly, though, there's an ideology behind a lot of marketers in the paid ad space that I fundamentally disagree with: because paid ads, from PPC to the Super Bowl, offer a short-term boost, they seem like a great investment. Unfortunately, they're a drug, and the more paid ads you purchase, the more you get hooked on them. Suddenly, you're committing giant marketing budgets to Google, Facebook, and ad buys while your house is crumbling in the background.

What I'm really getting at is this: if you're going to use paid ads, do so responsibly.

I genuinely believe that paid ads are only right for your company if you can check off all of these boxes:

- You possess an established and solid foundation for

your marketing efforts. Your brand assets, website, and database are all towards the top of your industry.

• You have a team hired that you can see growing with the company; there are no positions on your marketing staff that you'll want to hire for in the next three months.

• You have a respectable presence on third-party channels that you can attain for free.

• You have extensively tested the messaging and imagery on organic channels and have received mostly positive feedback.

• You are willing to commit a significant budget to paid ads in order to be competitive on any channel that you decide to play on.

If you've decided you're ready, turn the page. It's about to get fun.

Betting on the Right Paid Channels, and Avoiding the Wrong Ones

If you're ready to commit to the shotgun formation and the paid ads that come with it, then you're about to embark on a really fun part of your journey as a marketer. You've built the fire, and now you get to pour gasoline on it to get immediate returns for your efforts.

So, how do you figure out what channels are the best for you to gamble your budget on? The same way you find out anything: with a spreadsheet.

Keep this one simple—we don't want to get analysis paralysis. Every channel is going to inundate you with self-serving data. Don't get distracted by it.

Instead, focus on four key variables for each channel:

- **Is your target audience there?** Check yes or no.

- **What's the size of your target audience on that platform?** Get as specific as you can, and make sure that you're comparing apples-to-apples. If Facebook allows you to hyper target women between 35 and 40 who have bought a cat in the past year, don't compare those numbers to women over 30 who watch Oxygen.

- **What's the cost of each ad?** For traditional ads, you're looking at a per-placement cost whereas most digital ads will offer a price per click or a price per 1,000 impressions.

- **Finally, what do you need to make an impact?** This is more subjective than the other categories, but it's the most important factor of your decision. If you spend $1,000, will that saturate the channel, or barely get you noticed?

In the end, you should have a spreadsheet that lists the following variables for every channel you're considering.

- Channel

- Target Audience?

- Audience Size

- Unit Cost

- Test Budget Required

Once you've built this table out, you should have an easy assessment tool for paid channels. Be selective and choose wisely—you don't want to spread your resources too thin.

Instead, focus your test budget on participating in 1-3 paid channels extraordinarily well. Then, scale what works.

The Statue of Liberty Play Call: What About Direct Mail?

The Statue of Liberty is one of the most iconic trick plays in football, and it has led to some of the most exciting touchdowns in the history of the game. (2007 Fiesta Bowl, anyone?) The play is simple. The quarterback drops back as if he were to throw the ball. He pump fakes with his throwing arm while he hands the ball off to the running back with his off-hand. This tricks the defense into thinking the ball is being passed to one side of the field. Instead, the running back carries the ball easily into the end zone on the other side of the field.

To me, this is what direct mail represents in the marketing game, and that's why it's my favorite traditional marketing channel.

Most direct mail is a commodity. It's more or less an ad buy, a passing play. When put in the hands of an incredibly creative staff with a big enough budget, however, it can be turned into a run. Instead of blasting out a message or a coupon, you're offering value and creating a relationship.

Direct mail, especially true in the high-value sales B2B space, is perhaps the single greatest marketing channel for highly creative individuals. It's like the old guy at every pickup basketball game that seems like he's a step behind everyone—but you'll be darned if he doesn't have the best footwork and jump shot of anyone on the court.

To my fellow tech-heads, the idea that there's a place for low-budget direct mail pieces is practically treasonous. How dare I espouse anything other than digital marketing? Simple: **I have seen talented strategists create direct mail pieces that are more innovative than anything I've seen on any other channel in the ad space over the past five years.**

The creative license that you have with a big direct mail budget is unparalleled, your targeting can be extremely robust, and you can reach prospects that are unreachable on other channels.

You can send bourbon glasses to bourbon enthusiasts. You can send your pitch deck in a hand-etched wooden box with their name on it. You can come up with campaign-specific creative that makes a splash, or a timeless piece of swag that they'll keep in their office until the day they retire.

The only bad news about this? It costs... *big time*. We're talking $50 a piece.

Think about pizza coupon mailers. They'll do the job, but they're a commodity. There's nothing wrong with having them as a part of your portfolio, but they're basically banner ads that you printed out. If you're allocating more than 25% of your marketing spend to low-value direct mail, you're no better than the guy spending half of his budget on PPC.

The materials are going to be expensive, and you're going to want to hire a creative agency to do the job right. There's a time and there's a place, however, where that can be your absolute best bet.

If (*and only if*) you check all of the boxes below, it could be time to call up a creative agency and start talking about a big, expensive direct mail campaign.

- Our average sales price is big - Upwards of $50,000.

- Our average lifetime value of a customer is even bigger - Upwards of $100,000.

- Our primary decision makers are impossible to get on the phone and hard to reach via other channels.

- Our primary decision makers don't go to trade show floors, they send their lackeys for them.

- Our sales team deals primarily with gatekeepers and lower level staff members on their way up to trying to reach decision makers.

- Our industry is filled with noise and we haven't been able to bust through it on our own.

- We have a list of the people we want to reach, and we're positive that list is clean.

- We're willing to commit $50 on a direct mail piece to one person.

Completing the Pass: Wrapping Up Lead Generation

As I said in the beginning of this section, your lead generation's running and passing games need to work together in order to get the most potential sales opportunities for your business. Remember your central mission:

Marketing is about finding ways to communicate and connect your product to the everyday lives of consumers.

Think about your lead generation touch points—what are all the ways your customers can find you? Maybe that big potential sale you found at a trade show was unimpressed by your ineffectual email strategy. Or maybe that lone commenter on one of your blog posts turns out to be someone looking to open up a huge account or make a bulk product purchase.

By building a sustainable, balanced, two-pronged attack in your lead generation—using both patience in your content, email and social media, as well as seeking out more direct revenue channels—your offensive strategy can work as one to present a great, outward facing brand image to your entire audience.

Play Calls - Offense

Here's a list of things you can do today to improve
your team's offensive strategy.

◯ Identify and document the unique value that
your content can provide your marketplace.

◯ Create an email course for your email list
built around that unique value.

◯ Identify five third-party sources where your
brand could contribute. Reach out to them
to find out more about their guest
blogging policy.

◯ Research three paid advertising channels
that you believe could be a good fit for
your brand.

Sales Support: Your Invaluable Special Teams

In football, special teams players have a long history of going overlooked. They're often an after-thought by fans watching the game—but look closer and you'll see the amazing impact that special teams can have.

Whether it's Devin Hester opening the Super Bowl with kickoff return for a touchdown, Adam Vinateri hitting two Super Bowl winning field goals, or Auburn University's punt block team running back a missed field goal by their hated rival, the University of Alabama, for a 110-yard game winning touchdown, special teams can change the entire trajectory of a game's momentum.

Find a video clip of that last one online—it's ridiculous.

Similarly, one of the biggest mistakes you can make as you develop your marketing team is to ignore your sales team. Every marketer wants to build a high-powered offense or a tough defense, but few focus on the easy wins that you can get when you focus on sales.

Things like increasing closing rates, discovering more compelling case studies, and giving your sales team the tools that they need to be successful aren't as flashy as driving a ton of leads or building a sexy brand, but they are just as important. If you don't focus on them, you're leaving wins on the table.

In this section, we're going to discuss the value and importance of sales support. Too many marketers overlook this aspect of their job because it's not as fun as offense or defense, but the little things like understanding your team's sales process can go a long way in converting more leads and winning more games.

Bonus Section: Why You Should Never Make The Mistake Of Overlooking Special Teams

As a long-tortured fan of the Indianapolis Colts, however, I can tell you that your special teams can cost you as many games as your offense or defense if you don't invest in them.

Let's go through a brief history of my heartbreak.

It is the 2005 NFL season. The Indianapolis Colts, led by Peyton Manning, one of the greatest quarterbacks to ever play the game, march into the playoffs with a 14-2 record, the best in all of professional football. They have a first round bye, followed by a divisional round matchup with the Pittsburgh Steelers. We were playing at home, and we had already beaten this same Steelers team handily earlier in the season, so the fanbase wasn't too concerned about the outcome. Unfortunately, we got off to a sluggish start, and found ourselves down by three late in the fourth quarter.

After a miracle fumble recovery on our own one-yard line, we march down the field to set up a 42 yard field goal with 17 seconds remaining. Mike Vanderjagt, the most accurate field goal kicker in the history of professional football at this time, takes the field. He lines up the chip shot field goal to take us into overtime. The snap was good. The hold was good. The kick was wide, wide, wide right. That Steelers team would go on to win the Super Bowl—a Super Bowl that would have been ours, had it not been for our special teams.

Fast-forward a few years. Peyton Manning was having another year for the history books. After a rocky 3-4 start to the season, we rattled off nine straight wins to go into the playoffs as the hottest team in football with a three-time MVP leading the charge. Our first challenger was the San Diego Chargers in the Wild Card round of the playoffs. In this game, our offense outperformed theirs, beating them in total yards. Our defense forced two turnovers while their defense forced none. We looked like the heavy favorites, yet we lost. Why?

Mike *freaking* Scifres.

The Chargers' punter, Mike Scifres was the only player who

out-performed the Colts on that misty northern California night. He punted six times, netting an average of 51.7 yards, setting an NFL playoff record. Every punt of his was downed inside the 20 yard line. Two of them were downed inside the ten yard line. Most impressive, with just under three minutes remaining in the game and the league's MVP set to receive the ball with a three point lead, Scifres angled a punt out of bounds inside the one yard line.

For some writers, two examples would be enough, but this is my book and the Colts' special teams woes have haunted me for too long, so you have to read another.

The year is 2009 and the Indianapolis Colts are playing in the second Super Bowl of the Peyton Manning era. They had, once again, attained the best record in the NFL behind Manning's leadership, and went into the Super Bowl favored to defeat the New Orleans Saints. After taking a 10-6 lead into the locker room, with both talent and momentum on their side, they started the second half by receiving the ball.

Or so they thought.

Instead of kicking off, the Saints attempted an onside kick to start the third quarter. This took the Colts by surprise, with the ball bouncing off of the facemask of Colts player Hank Baskett. The Saints recovered the kick and went on to outscore the Colts 25-7 throughout the rest of the game. This was the first onside kick ever recovered outside of the fourth quarter in NFL history.

So there you have it. Special teams may have cost Peyton Manning three Super Bowls. This isn't an afterthought for great coaches—it's an area that requires great consideration and discipline. While offense and defense tend to dominate the discussion, the best coaches know that in order to win a championship, your special teams personnel need to play at the highest possible level.

Marketing Qualified Leads, Revenue, and Wins

Building a future-proof digital ecosystem is a wonderful goal, but if you're not generating revenue, you may not be around long enough to see your future-proof ecosystem grow.

One of your most important jobs as a marketer is to consistently deliver marketing qualified leads and revenue. These are ultimately the metrics that your entire department will be judged on. It's also where the relationship between marketing and sales becomes extremely important. By the transitive property, that means your success and failure is literally dependent on the relationship with your sales team.

For many marketers, this is a harsh reality. They don't want to focus on working hand-in-hand with their sales team, they want to hand off leads and tell the sales department to smile and dial.

This approach cannot, and will not succeed in the 21st century for a few reasons:

- Your prospect's experience will feel siloed, undermining the relationship that your marketing materials and lead nurturing efforts have tried to build.

- Your sales staff will have to constantly swim upstream, trying to convert warm prospects without the right kinds of information to tee up conversations.

- Your marketing staff will begin to diverge from your sales staff in message, tone, and objective, meaning that your marketing and sales messaging will become more disparate.

Solving this problem is simple, and it requires working on the same team with your sales department to achieve common objectives. Once you've aligned your sales and marketing efforts, then you can worry about additional metrics, objectives, and key performance indicators.

Getting on the Same Page with Your Sales Team

This process requires humility and grace. If you're new to an organization, you can play dumb. If you've been in the organization for a while, however, you may have already had some spats with the sales department.

This is incredibly common within companies, but overcoming this issue isn't as simple as aligning goals.

Tell your Director of Sales that you'd like to set a meeting so you can better understand their department's objectives. Approach this meeting with an open-mind, and be willing to admit you're wrong, even if you think you're right. If you've had trouble delivering "qualified" leads in the past, then approach that issue head on, and find out what you can do to solve the problem.

In this meeting, you want to ask the following questions:

- What does the sales process look like?

- What qualifying questions does the sales team ask of prospects?

- What pain points do sales personnel look for?

- What does a "qualified" lead look like?

- What common characteristics do the best customers have?

- What things do the sales team members look for to indicate a person is likely to close?

- What does the sales team like about the leads they've gotten from the marketing team in the past?

- What does the sales team dislike about the leads they've gotten from the marketing team in the past?

- What aspects of the sales process does the marketing team understand well?

- What aspects of the sales process doesn't the marketing team understand?

- If you were to create a list of qualifying conditions for every lead we send to the sales team, would the Director of Sales be willing to look it over and give you feedback?

From that meeting forward, it's your responsibility to establish a list of qualifying conditions for a lead to be considered "Marketing Qualified" before being handed off to the sales team.

Ideally, these conditions are things like:

- Expressed interest in a demo on a form.

- Identified a problem that they're looking to solve on a form.

- Have a lead score of X based on Y conditions that we have agreed are important.

These conditions should NOT be things like:

- Downloaded a recent E-Guide.

- Viewed our pricing page.

- Subscribed to our email list.

This is a common misstep for marketers. They want more MQLs to pad their numbers. Resist this urge and keep your focus on delivering warm leads with meaningful information to your sales team.

Once your Director of Sales has agreed on what a "qualified" lead looks like, you can move on to measuring other key performance indicators.

Seeing the World Like Your Sales Team

In marketing circles, we love metrics. We talk about MQLs, SQLs, Marketing Qualified Revenue, and conversion rates. We talk about how much potential revenue is in the pipeline, and we *think* that we're speaking the same language as our sales team.

After all, they follow up on leads, and they like revenue. So if we talk about how many leads we give them and how much revenue we help them make, we're all on the same page.

No, actually you're not.

Your sales team has a much different perspective. Their job isn't to be focused on the big, high-level numbers. Their job is to make plays, and making plays on special teams will win you games.

Unfortunately, not every play on special teams can be as

momentous as that huge Auburn runback (seriously, have you watched that yet?), and if your only focus as a marketer is trying to force plays and strategy instead of putting them in positions to succeed, you're not only doing them a disservice, but you could be actively damaging your overall business.

In sales support, just like in special teams, there are plenty of possibilities for any potential sale.

Sometimes, effective sales support will put your defense in a great position. Other times, effective sales support will put your offense in striking distance for a score. Sometimes it's a whole team effort, and your sales staff will close a deal that they couldn't have otherwise without the proper support. Your sales support will rarely make headlines, but it can win games for you and it can *definitely* lose games for you if you neglect it.

Understanding the Sales Process

Here's a fun game to play: next time you're talking to a Marketing Director, ask him what sales training his sales team has gone through. About half of the time, he'll have no idea, and unfortunately, ignorance is *not* a virtue here.

It doesn't matter how great you are at your job—until you have a deep understanding of your sales staff's process, you will never deliver them the right leads consistently.

The only way to overcome this obstacle is with transparency and communication. It's not enough to have a couple meetings where you ask about their needs. You need to get involved. You need to see them in action. You need to understand their best and worst moments on the job, as well as find out what their biggest fears are when they pick up the phone.

It's not easy, but it's absolutely necessary for your success. No matter the size or shape of your organization, this should always go through the following process:

Start By Shadowing

The only way to understand the sales process is to see it in action. Throughout your interfacing with the Director of Sales at your company, make sure you have a firm understanding of the following:

- What's your sales methodology? What formal training (if any) has the sales team gone through?

- What does an ideal client look like?

- What does an ideal first call look like?

- What common objections does the team have to overcome?

- What competitors does the sales team most commonly lose deals to?

- What are the biggest deal breakers that prospects bring up?

- What are the most common selling points that close deals?

- What do you wish the sales team was better equipped to handle?

- Who are the three top performers in the sales department?

Shadowing Your Sales Team

Next, you should shadow the top three salespeople recommended to you in the last question.

Ask to shadow them on a day when they have a variety of calls scheduled. Ideally, you want to see them in at least one first call and at least one potential close. This will give you a better understanding of what they need throughout their entire sales cycle.

When they're on the phone, pay special attention to the following:

- What questions does the salesperson ask? Why? What are they trying to accomplish with each?

- What questions does the prospect ask? How does the salesperson answer? Are there any answers that he seems uneasy with?

- What types of leads result in smooth conversations? What types of leads are more difficult or hostile?

While you're shadowing each salesperson, you also want to find downtime to build rapport and better understand their voice and tone. Understanding how they communicate and view the world, will help you build your messaging around what's working for clients.

Make sure to ask questions about each salesperson's best clients and biggest wins. Try to understand their best-case scenarios, and their easiest sales. The better you understand what an easy win looks like to them, the more effectively you can deliver easy wins to their inbox.

While you're at it, don't shy away from worst-case scenarios either. You need to understand what they're afraid of when they pick up the phone if you want to put those fears to rest.

Make It All About Them

Throughout this entire process, you want to make it all about them. You're the quarterback calling the plays, but they're the receiver that ultimately scores the touchdown.

Your job is to facilitate them, not compete with them. You want to make them feel supported, respected, and empowered. You want them to be the star of the show and the captain of your industry. *They're* the hero of the story, while *you're* the lovable sidekick.

Seeing the Whole Playing Field

As you can see, effective digital marketing requires a game-plan that fires on multiple levels—combining great defense, offense, and special teams.

With solid, foundational brand messaging and voice, a balanced approach to lead generation and content, along with a sales team with the tools they need to succeed, there's no limit to what your marketing efforts can accomplish.

Now, get ready to put on your "General Manager" hat, as we take an even further step back to see the big picture of your marketing efforts, and truly put the "future" in future-proofing.

Play Calls - Special Teams

Here's a list of things you can do today to establish solid a
solid special teams effort in your department.

- Schedule a meeting with your Director of
  Sales to discuss definitions of terms like
  "qualified leads."

- Schedule interviews with your sales team to
  better understand areas where they could
  use more assistance.

- Make a list of three things that you will do in
  the next quarter to provide more support to
  your sales team.

Part 3

BEING THE GM:

Nurturing Your Sustainable Marketing Ecosystem

"When you come to the fork in the road, take it."

— Yogi Berra, on the importance of
adapting to new digital marketing technologies

To the casual observer, the rise of the 2016 Chicago Cubs seemed meteoric. This is a team that was only a few years removed from mediocrity that was now competing for the franchise's first World Series since 1908. If you're friends with any diehard Cubs fans, however, you saw this coming from a mile away.

> *"Everything's okay. Our farm system is looking GOOD!"*
>
> — My friend Michael, every day since 2011

See, the Cubs' General Manager, Theo Epstein, had built a system and had been testing the pieces of that system in the minor leagues for five years before the Cubs rose to greatness. He could have gone out, spent a lot of money, and tried to generate short-term success, but instead he opted to take his time and build a system that could sustain success over the long-term.

That's how you build a future-proof franchise. You don't build around stars you just signed. You don't throw rookies into the starting lineup on day one. You selectively test every single one of your players in a single-A league, then AA, then you test them in AAA, then you give them a shot in the Major Leagues, and then, if they're still working out, they become a part of your regular rotation.

Similarly, in marketing, tacticians love to jump from channel-to-channel, finding new and inventive ways to spend their budget. This is great if it's done with the big picture in mind, but allocating too much time, energy, and money to emerging channels can hurt the bottom line as you spend more money in the proving grounds than you do once you've perfected marketing on a given channel.

In this section, we will discuss how to systematically attack new and emerging marketing channels. We'll talk about how templates can simplify your approach to new channels, what metrics to follow as you test new channels, and how you can test new strategies in the minor leagues before you spend the time, energy, and budget necessary to work them into your Major League rotation.

Building From Your Formations: The Magic of Marketing Strategy Templates

Coaches love to tweak their playbook in the offseason, but it would be exhausting to build plays and sets from scratch every time, which is why most coaches focus on a core group of formations that they already know and trust, then make changes from there.

Similarly, building a rock solid marketing strategy is difficult. Creating one every month or every quarter to ensure that you stay ahead of the curve for years to come can seem daunting to even the most experienced marketing directors.

By using a simple template, however, this effort can become much more manageable.

This leaves many marketers with a predicament. Where do I get a marketing strategy template? Do I build one myself or download one off the Internet? Should I ask around, or keep this to myself?

With a little bit of research, you should be able to build

your own marketing strategy template in a matter of days, allowing you to save weeks worth of work over the course of your career.

Continue to Assess Your Business Objectives

The first thing you need to do is take a step back and assess what business objectives you're trying to achieve with your marketing strategy as it pertains to the "big picture." How is what you're doing now going to affect what you're going to be doing five years from now?

Too often, marketers make the mistake of not aligning their goals with the company's growth, or expected growth.

Luckily, correcting this problem is easy. By continuing to work with everyone from your executives to your sales staff, you'll be able to figure out how you can align your goals directly to their goals, both now and into the future. If your sales team wants more leads, include that as a KPI. If your executives want to see more brand visibility or want to explore a new vertical, incorporate these goals into your strategy. This is the single most important step to building an effective strategy, and it needs to be incorporated into your template.

Next, assess what tools you have at your disposal. Part of your business objective is going to be controlling costs, so understanding what you can do in-house and what you need to hire a marketing agency for is important. Make a list of everything you can accomplish in-house and everything you'll need to outsource. If you can estimate costs effectively, include this as well.

Find the Right Platforms for Your Future Marketing Efforts

Next, you need to figure out where you want to execute. Do you want to build a strong digital marketing strategy and ignore more traditional channels? Or would you rather eschew digital in favor of the tried and true mediums you've been using for years?

Here are a few questions you should ask when determining what platforms to use in your strategy document:

- What platforms have we tried in the past? What worked? What didn't?

- What platforms do our customers live on? Are they likely to look online for answers to their questions, or would they rather be communicated via more traditional methods?

- How can we re-purpose content that we're already creating? If we do a quarterly email newsletter, could we also turn that into a blog post or direct mail piece? How can we get more results from one piece of marketing?

- Where do our salespeople meet our customers? Are they more likely to be at networking events or adding each other on LinkedIn?

- What can I test at a low cost? The easiest way to figure out what works is by testing it! I recommend testing one new platform a quarter just to see what works.

All of these are questions that you can continue assessing on a regular basis to assure that you're keeping up with the most current information about your company's various departments, as well as your client or customer base.

Build a Marketing Strategy Template That Can Last For Years

The whole purpose of a template is to have an asset that you can reuse for years to come. It's important, therefore, to follow a general outline that won't deviate much from month-to-month or quarter-to-quarter.

Here's a general outline that I like to follow for many of my marketing strategy documents:

Introduction

Traditional Marketing Strategy Overview

- Traditional Channel 1

- Traditional Channel 2

- Traditional Channel 3

Digital Marketing Strategy Overview

- Digital Channel 1

- Digital Channel 2

- Digital Channel 3

Outcomes and Objectives

- Primary Goals – Marketing Department

- Primary Goals/KPI's – Rest of the Organization

Resources Needed

Building a digital marketing strategy template is a great way to provide more insight into the process for those who are curious. If you need to incorporate more specifics, start looking at individual platforms you plan on using to elaborate even further.

Once you've built an effective marketing strategy template, you should be able to rinse and repeat, effectively re-using this document for years. Think of it like the way you assess incoming prospects, or win potential down the line. It's all about re-contextualizing industry changes or trends into standardized constructs by which your team can measure success.

Some sections may change dramatically through the years while others remain virtually unchanged, but the amount of time and energy you'll need to put into your strategy will be reduced substantially.

Tracing Revenue and Measuring KPI's Like a Minor League Scout

Teams track tons of in-game stats, and advanced stats have provided teams with more insights into their team than ever. While organizations that have embraced big data have thrived, there's a dirty little secret that most people aren't talking about.

This optimization is happening around the margins. In the MLB, for example, they absolutely need to be leveraging advanced statistics to perfect their strategy, but in the minor leagues, simply measuring base-line stats will get them where they need to be.

Revenue attribution and KPI measurement can get extremely

wonky, especially as you try using it to future-proof your marketing efforts for years to come. Some marketers, myself included, like to dive really deep into things like multi-touch attribution.

This is great, but it's overkill for small and medium-sized organizations. It also varies so dramatically from organization to organization, that I can't really speak intelligently about what a multi-touch attribution plan would look like for you.

Instead, I recommend most businesses start with a more stripped down attribution model that can then be expanded upon as they grow in size and sophistication.

This approach involves breaking out your various marketing activities into four categories—Brand Awareness, Lead Generation, Lead Nurturing, and Generating Referrals—and assigning between one and three KPIs to each activity depending on the category's importance.

The result may look something like this:

Brand Awareness

- Twitter - Increase following by 10%

- Facebook - Increase engagement levels by 25%

- Podcast - Increase our average weekly listens by 50%

Lead Generation

- Content Marketing - Increase web traffic by 20%

- Content Marketing - Increase conversion rate by 50%

- Tradeshows - Generate 500 MQLs at tradeshows
this quarter

Lead Nurturing

- Email Marketing - Increase our email open rate by 25%

- Email Marketing - Generate 1,200 MQLs from email
marketing this quarter

- Direct Mail - Generate $500,000 in revenue from direct

mail campaigns this quarter

Generating Referrals

- Referral program - Acquire 100 new customers from referrals this quarter

You'll notice a few common threads in the goals set above.

First and foremost, they're all quantifiable. It's extremely important to set measurable goals, even if you miss them. The only way that you can build a marketing department that routinely hits its goals is by building a marketing department that routinely measures its activity.

Second, you'll notice that the further down you go the more the metrics focus on revenue. This is intentional. You can measure ROI on things like social media or podcasting, but it's extremely time consuming. If you're a large company, especially in the B2C space, then multi-touch attribution across social channels could be extremely important, but it's more important not to conflate ROI with success.

In most cases, you're better served making a lasting brand impression on social media than making a sale, so quit trying to measure all channels with the same metrics.

Tracking the Next Big Thing: the Future of User Behavior Data

Hopefully by now you understand the big picture importance of user behavior data to the future of digital marketing, and you know it's only going to double down as we look beyond these current updates.

While we can't peek behind the curtain with Hummingbird or any future Google algorithm update, we do know that user behavior data is a vital component of *how* Hummingbird interprets SERPs. This is a vital realization for SEO success in 2016 and beyond.

Here are four simple steps to improving your user behavior data as you turn your marketing focus to the years ahead:

1. **Track your current bounce rate across all pages:** Knowing you have a problem is the first step, right? Track

your bounce rate and average time on page across all pages in Google Analytics. Pay attention to what kinds of pages have the best and worst numbers.

2. Ensure every page has unique meta-information: Dig into each page's meta description and title to ensure that they're enticing people to click. Including target keywords is important to improving click-through rate.

3. Check your on-page experience for your top 5 keywords: Go search for those target keywords you want to rank for. How does your site look compared to your competition? Is your user experience worse? If so, you'll likely see a lot of people pogo-sticking.

4. Always be testing: Never stop testing new meta descriptions, titles, and user experience options. I've seen tests that double our click-through rate and I've seen tests that have no effect. The worst thing you can do is nothing!

Once you've mastered the basics of leveraging user behavior data, you can continue learning and adjusting to ensure that you stay on the cutting edge in the field—and that you stay off

Google's blacklist.

Using Google's Rule Book to Your Advantage

So, now that we know the importance of user behavior data, and we're keeping an eye on our site's user behavior data, how do we take advantage of Google's rulebook?

Here is a brief rundown of things you should do to understand how Google views your site:

- Continuously check your website's speed with Google's PageSpeed Insights. If your site is showing up in the red, you need to upgrade immediately.

- Get your site registered with Google Search Console. This allows you to optimize your site's search performance.

- Register your business with Google My Business and optimize it for the Knowledge Graph. Don't be afraid to use lots of pictures!

- Create lists of target keywords with Google's Keyword Planner tool.

- Finally, when in doubt, search for keywords you want to rank well for and assess your competition. What sites look good? What sites look dated? This should help you assess your positioning within the competitive landscape.

Maintaining an Effective Backlink Profile

We got into this a little bit when talking about third party media opportunities, but depending on your industry and circumstance, there could be a dozen different reasons that you need to closely monitor your backlink profile.

If you're a large corporation, it can be difficult to keep an eye on all relevant stakeholders with your website. All it takes is one vendor leveraging black hat tactics to get your site penalized permanently. If you're a small company with a small number of backlinks, it'll be pretty easy for your competition to hire someone nefarious to sink your site with fraudulent link spamming.

The bad news is that no website is safe from ignorant or nefarious backlinks. The good news is that this problem is extremely preventable if you're proactive about it.

SEO, Sender Score, and various reputation monitors on social media can lead to death from a thousand paper cuts. I've never seen one bad backlink ruin a website. Usually, it's *hundreds* of bad backlinks.

"But Tim, I can always disavow them!"

First and foremost, Google is way smarter than you are. You're not tricking Larry Page with your "disavowed" backlink spam. Secondly, these problems are easily preventable, so long as you know what to look for.

Here's a simple task list that will help you monitor and prevent backlink issues from ruining your website:

- **Perform a complete backlink audit on your website.** There are dozens of great tools that do this, but I recommend Moz to my clients. This is the most time consuming part of the process, but if you do this right the first time, it will save you hours down the road.

- **Identify all potential spam risks and disavow them immediately.** The reason I recommend Moz for backlink checking is because they make this process so easy. Simply go to their "Spam Analysis" tab and export a disavow file of all links above a certain spam score. You will then want to closely review that document to ensure that you actually want to disavow all those links, then upload that into Google's Webmaster Tools.

• **Set up a Google alert for your specific URL.** Any time your URL is mentioned or linked to, Google will automatically email you. I recommend setting this alert to send once a day. Also, consider setting up a Google alert for any mention of your brand name and/or other brand-specific keywords. This may help you identify things that fall through the cracks with other tools.

• **Run a quarterly backlink audit to ensure that everything pointing back to your website is on the up-and-up.** There will always be a few sketchy backlinks pointing to any site, but by auditing this regularly, you can prevent that ratio from getting out of control.

How to Leverage Multivariate Testing to Perfect Your Marketing Efforts

There's a reason baseball sends its newest prospects down to the minors first before promoting them up to the major leagues—they need to be properly tested to see if they can help the big club before the organization invests more serious time and money in them.

In addition to betting on the right channels, it's extremely important to test your ads extensively in each channel. I believe that unless you're willing to run multivariate tests on your ads and marketing campaigns, you're not doing your job.

Now, testing your marketing is an interesting challenge because there's no standard definition as to what constitutes a "test." What one marketer considers a "test" another marketer in the same industry may write off. On the other hand, some tests run by advanced marketers wouldn't even be recognizable to their less experienced counterparts.

When testing your marketing strategies and channels, it's important to understand your limitations. Plenty of marketers aren't ready to jump into multivariate testing, and that's fine! For those marketers, there are always other options to hit first before graduating to the ropes course.

Different Ways to Test Your Marketing

If you're looking for some more basic approaches to test your marketing, try the following:

- Basic Experiments: A basic experiment is the simplest test you can run with your marketing. When running a basic experiment, all you're doing is trying something new for a statistically significant period of time, I recommend 1-2 months. A good example of a basic experiment would be changing the "From" address on your marketing emails from your company to an individual on your team.

- Platform Tests: When experimenting with a new platform, a basic experiment isn't enough. If you want to find out whether a new social network is a good fit for your brand, you need to commit to testing it for at least 3-6 months. This includes things like Twitter, Facebook, email and blogging (we'll explore how to vet new marketing channels in a moment).

• A/B/C/D/E Tests: This is where things get interesting. Once you're ready to start diving into large-scale testing, you can experiment with A/B experiments. This means that you can send an email with two different subjects to two similar lists to see which performs best. This is the baby step that leads to multivariate testing.

• **Basic Experiments:** A basic experiment is the simplest test you can run with your marketing. When running a basic experiment, all you're doing is trying something new for a statistically significant period of time, I recommend 1-2 months. A good example of a basic experiment would be changing the "From" address on your marketing emails from your company to an individual on your team.

• **Platform Tests:** When experimenting with a new platform, a basic experiment isn't enough. If you want to find out whether a new social network is a good fit for your brand, you need to commit to testing it for at least 3-6 months. This includes things like Twitter, Facebook, email and blogging (we'll explore how to vet new marketing channels in a moment).

• **A/B/C/D/E Tests:** This is where things get interesting. Once you're ready to start diving into large-scale testing, you can experiment with A/B experiments. This means that you can send an email with two different subjects to two similar lists to see which performs best. This is the baby step that leads to multivariate testing.

How to Use Multivariate Testing in Emails

Once you're ready to start multivariate testing, you'll never want to stop. Unfortunately, most major marketing automation platforms don't have multivariate testing built-in. This means that you need to do it yourself.

The good news is that it's not as hard as it sounds...

• Export your email list as a .csv and open it in Excel.

• Add a new column A.

• Type in "=RANDBETWEEN(1,1000000)", fill the

entire row.

- Sort Column A smallest to largest.

- Delete Column A.

- Divide this list as you see fit. If you're testing 5 variations, split it into 5 lists, etc.

- Upload these lists into the software you use to manage
your email.

- Send a unique variation of your email to each of
these lists.

A couple important notes here...

First, it's important that you have a "baseline" for your test
that can serve as your "standard operating email"—like a
control group in a science experiment. This shouldn't be
anything—it's just an email like any other you'd send. Once
you have this baseline, only change one thing about it per
test email.

Once you hit send, you can measure your results by individual list in order to understand what variation is most effective. For best results, try 2-3 times per list to ensure one isn't abnormally responsive.

How to Use Multivariate Testing in Digital Ads

Digital ads can be vexing for a lot of marketers because there's so little to work with. By limiting headline copy to 25 characters and putting strict requirements on imagery, Facebook and Google seem to get a kick out of eliminating creativity from ads.

That being said, this can make digital ads one of the most effective mediums for multivariate testing.

For all my ads, I create 5 headlines, 5 bodies and 5 images. Then, I mix and match every permutation of these elements until I have over 100 ads. This allows me to test each variable independently.

It's not glamorous or easy, but the results are phenomenal.

How to Use Multivariate Testing on Your Website

If you're committing time and money driving people to your website, you might want to start testing the pages people land on in order to ensure that you're not missing any opportunities once they arrive. Personally, I like to use Optimizely on all of my headlines and calls to action in order to get a better understanding of what language resonates with my target market.

Vetting and Adding Future Channels to Your Farm System

If you've done everything to this point, congratulations! You now have a brand, marketing strategy, and digital presence that is resilient enough to handle whatever the future holds.

Soon, however, you'll most certainly be faced with the choice to add future channels and resources to your strategy— things beyond the present purview of this book.

For every social network, there are a select few marketers courageous enough to test it out before anyone else. Some succeed while others make complete fools of themselves. When Snapchat first arrived on the scene, for example, not even its creators had a solid understanding of how marketers could leverage the platform.

Nevertheless, you saw dozens of marketers rush to squat on their brand name and start posting pictures and videos, as if it were Instagram. We also saw a few marketers focus on more interesting functionality, like temporary coupons that customers could only use while they were in their story, or custom geofilters for their unique location.

How can you avoid the former while still getting in the ring to compete for a chance at the latter?

First and foremost, treat every new channel the same way we discussed treating paid ads—very carefully, like a sometimes snack for your marketing strategy. It's simply too risky to assume that the platform will be around forever if it's only been around for a couple of years.

Second, I have a simple audit that I perform for every new channel I consider. Steal this. Make it your own. You'll be able to identify new channels that fit your brand, avoid the new channels that don't, and look smarter when your boss asks you what you know about WhatsApp.

New Channel Audit

- What is it? What does it do?

- What current platform(s) is it most similar to? What makes it unique?

- Who are the typical users on this platform? How do they align with your target market?

- What revenue generating opportunities does this platform present?

- How can you use this platform to drive web traffic and grow your audience?

- How can this platform help us improve your thought leadership efforts?

- What type of content tends to resonate the most with

the users of this platform, and what "unique take" do you have on that type of content?

- How much time would that content take to produce a week?

By performing this simple audit, you can easily assess how likely it is that you'll be able to use this new platform to your advantage.

Stay Nimble, Stay Successful

As we've discussed throughout this book, it's extremely important that your marketing team remain nimble enough to react to changes in the market.

In addition to an agile management structure, you need to keep a pulse on your customers, and your competition, so that you can react to the market.

To that end, I recommend using a few digital tools to create a virtual dashboard of competitive research. Simply identify 3-5 key competitors, set up the listening tools, design a dashboard to keep track of all of your information, then update it once every two weeks for your sprint planning session.

This will allow you to spot opportunities as they arise and identify threats before they can have an impact on your business.

Use the following tools to monitor your competitive landscape:

Google Forms

This is your single most valuable tool. It allows you to build a form that you can use to collect regular feedback. Send this to everyone in your organization and ask them to fill it out any time they hear news, good or bad, about a competitor. This should include:

- Competitor's Name (Drop Down Menu)

- What Have You Heard?

- Link(s) if relevant

- Files/Screenshots if relevant

- Would you characterize this as a positive, negative, or neutral development for our competitor?

- Notes or other comments

Google Alerts

Set up Google Alerts for the following:

- Your key competition's company name

- Your key competition's executive team's names

- Your company name

- Your executive team's names

Sprout Social

Set up social media listening on Sprout Social, Hootsuite, or a similar tool for the following:

- Your key competition's company name

- Your key competition's executive team's names

- Your company name

- Your executive team's names

- Your key competition's company account(s)

- Your key competition's executive team's account(s)

- Your company's account(s)

- Your executive team's account(s)

This puts you in the driver's seat and allows you to update your dashboard once a sprint to reflect the changing competitive landscape. It also gives you a better understanding of the discrepancy between your competition's public and private perception.

Monitoring Your Farm System

A great farm system in baseball patiently assesses its young prospects to fit them into their big picture vision for the team, so a great GM isn't thinking about how the team will win tonight—they're thinking about how they'll win three years from now.

As a marketer, it's your job to balance this approach when possible, and use all the tools at your disposal to decide how your brand and essence of today will grow and adapt in the ever-changing world of digital marketing.

By staying nimble, creating templates, using multivariate analysis, vetting new channels effectively, and keeping your eye towards how everything will fit into your user experience, you'll be able to use all your resources, staff, and expertise to ensure your marketing efforts are future-proofed for years to come.

Play Calls - Being the GM

Here's a list of things you can do today to improve your standing as a general manager.

- ✓ Document clear, measurable goals for the next quarter of marketing activities.

- ✓ Create a reporting template that you can present to your boss at the end of the quarter.

- ✓ Identify three emerging channels that you think would be compelling areas for growth next year.

CONCLUSION:

What to Do When the Future Happens

"A good hockey player plays where the puck is.
A great hockey player plays where the puck is going."

— Wayne Gretzky, giving advice to young
digital marketers while using hockey as a metaphor

The very first banner ad was run on October 27th, 1994. That means, as of this book's publication, digital advertising is 22 years old.

And like most 22 year olds, it's time for it to get its act together.

To date, digital advertising has been dominated by near-sighted, short-term thinking. Immediate return on investment has trumped long term, sustainable growth. Over the past few years, however, marketing giants like Jay Baer, Seth Godin, and Gary Vaynerchuk have ushered in a new way of thinking.

Instead of demanding the same instant gratification from our search marketing as consumers require for their search results, it's time that we find a more moderate road. It's time that we build long-term, sustainable assets that will deliver us value in 10 years, rather than continuously burning through money on quick hits.

The title of this book may have been a misnomer. There really isn't any one marketing strategy that is future-proof, but the playbook I've laid out in these pages is about as close to it as you can get. This is a playbook being run by successful marketing strategists around the world, leaving shortsighted tacticians behind.

The tactics have changed in the past five years, and they'll change again in the next five years, but the fundamental principles remain the same:

1. Start by building the things you own. Get your house in order before you try to grow.

2. Grow moderately. Test things like messages, imagery, and ideas for free before you dump tons of money into ads.

3. Test everything rigorously and don't be afraid to let your pet project die when the results come back negative.

4. Once you've found something that works, dump gasoline on the fire.

5. Audit yourself and your competitors regularly, so the future never catches you off guard.

Ten years from now, design trends will change, ranking

factors will be different, new social networks will come, and old social networks will die—but a few things will always stay the same.

You always want to be learning. You always want to be growing. You always want to be faster. You always want to be better. Everything else is fleeting.

Thank you so much for taking the time to read this book. It's been an absolute pleasure sharing my ideas with you.

Now, let's play ball.

GLOSSARY

Acronyms, Jargon, & Words You Should Know

2x2 Matrix

An easy way to visualize a competitive marketplace based on two variables. For example, you can have an X-Axis that reads "cost" and a Y-Axis that reads "quality." You then chart all of your competitors on that matrix.

A

Agency

Company that provides marketing or development services to other companies. Individuals who work for these companies are said to be "Agency-side.

Agile Marketing

An iterative management structure designed to help departments easily pivot based on results and market feedback.

Alexa Ranking

A ranking system that measures every website in the world based on average traffic. Alexa is owned by Amazon.

Alt-Text

"Alternative text," a description that you give to imagery on your website so Google knows how to index those images.

B

B2B

Business to Business, any business where the end result is a business buying a product or service.

B2C

Business to Consumer, any business where the end result is an individual buyer purchasing a product.

Backlink

A link back to your website from another webpage.

Backlink Profile

A holistic view of all of the backlinks you have pointed to your site.

Black Hat/Grey Hat Tactics

Tactics used in digital marketing, especially SEO, that are considered to be spammy or illegitimate. If it seems too easy, it's probably black hat.

Blacklisting
The process of banning a domain from a platform, usually used in search.

Brand Voice
How your company talks. Your brand's unique perspective on business, your marketplace, and your product.

Body Text
The main text of a web page or blog post. Usually surrounded by a <body> tag.

Bottom-Funnel
Leads who are close to a purchasing decision.

Bounce Rate
The percent of visitors who leave your website after viewing only one page.

C

Click-Through Rate
The percent of people who click on a link on a piece of marketing. This is used in PPC, Google Analytics, and Email Marketing to name a few.

CMO
Chief Marketing Officer.

Consumer Touch Point
Any interaction that a consumer or prospect has with your brand.

Color Palette
The colors that your brand uses. Usually divided into primary colors (your brand's main colors), secondary colors (colors that work well with your primary colors) and tertiary colors (colors that can be used in special circumstances).

CPC
Cost-Per-Click, a system through which you're charged every time a user clicks on an advertisement.

CPM

Cost-Per-Impression, a system through which you're charged for every 1,000 impressions your advertisement gets on a website.

D

Data Hygiene

The process of keeping your data free of errors, duplication, and unnecessary information.

Digital PR

The process of building relationships with bloggers and leveraging them to get featured on niche websites and publications.

Disavowing Links

The process through which you can tell Google that a spammy backlink is erroneous and should not penalize your website.

Distribution Channel

A method of distributing your product, such as in-store or online.

Domain Authority

A measure of a website's strength online. Several websites have recipes to determine this, but I trust Moz's Domain Authority as the most accurate.

Double Opt-In

The process of asking users to confirm twice that they want to receive messages from you.

E

EdgeRank

An algorithm that Facebook uses to prioritize the content that you want to see in your newsfeed.

Email Automation

A system that sends email marketing messages to new prospects automatically, in a sequence, after they've signed up for your email list.

Experian Data

Information collected by Experian on target prospects. This includes extremely robust psychographic profiles and troves of financial data.

F

First-Party Media

Media channels that you own, such as your blog.

First-Party Distribution

Distribution channels that you own, such as a store on your website.

Funnel Optimization

The process of ensuring that you're converting all prospects in your funnel to customers at the highest rate possible.

G

Google Keyword Research Tool

A tool provided by Google to help you research keywords to target in Google AdWords campaigns or in SEO efforts.

Google Pagespeed Insights

A tool provided by Google to help you see how your website performs on desktop and mobile.

Graphic Designer

A visual communicator that combines images, words, and ideas to convey information to an audience.

Growth Hacking

A term used to describe marketers who use unconventional means to achieve organizational growth.

H

H1/H2/H3

Heading tags used in blog posts and web pages in order to denote the site's content hierarchy.

HTML Email Template

What a developer creates for an organization so that they can send branded email messages to their email list.

I

In-House

How you describe a marketer who is employed by the organization he or she is marketing for.

K

KPIs

Key Performance Indicators, or metrics that marketers use to measure success.

L

Lead Nurturing

The process of sending tailored messages to marketing leads in order to convert them to sales.

Loading Javascript Asynchronously

This is a process which allows full websites to load without render-blocking Javascript slowing down the process. Javascript only loads after the rest of the website has completed loading.

M

Marketing Qualified Leads (MQLs)

Leads that the marketing department believes are qualified enough to be passed on to sales.

Marketing Qualified Revenue

Revenue that the marketing department believes they had a hand in generating.

Middle-Funnel

These prospects are considered to be in the "Interest" or "Desire" phase of purchasing. They might be interested in your product, but they aren't quite ready to buy.

Modular Design

This is a design framework that creates websites, apps, and products in a systematic fashion to build on one another. Rather than creating one web page, you create several building blocks that can be mixed and matched to create hundreds of web pages.

Multivariate Testing

Testing several variables at once, usually used in PPC, but can also be used for things like landing page optimization.

O

Organic Search

How users find your website if they Google a phrase and find you as a result.

P

PageRank

An outdated metric, created by Google, to measure the authority of web pages.

Pages/Session

The number of web pages the average user views on your website every time they visit.

Panda

A search filter introduced in February 2011 meant to stop sites with poor quality content from attaining high search rankings.

Penguin
A search filter introduced in April 2012 to better catch sites deemed to be spamming its search results, usually through paid link building.

Pingdom
A website that helps you determine your website's overall performance.

Pogo-Sticking
When users search a phrase, click on a result, and then hit the back button to return to the search page.

PPC
Price-Per-Click, how much platforms charge for ads in a PPC system.

Promotions Tab
An email inbox view created by Google to filter out all promotional messages from companies.

Preview Text

The text that shows up at the very beginning of an email in the inbox view. Usually the first line of an email.

Price Sensitivity

Users who are highly price-sensitive are less likely to buy as the cost of a product or service goes up.

Progressive Enhancement

A development framework that builds for the lowest-common-denominator first. This means that, if technology changes, is blocked, or is not yet available for a user, their website will still load and function.

R

Rebranding Exercise

A group activity that you do with your team in order to better understand what your brand means to them.

Referral Program

A system designed to reward current customers for referring new customers to your product or service.

Render-blocking Javascript

Javascript that must load before the rest of your website can be loaded.

ROI

Return on Investment, a constant metric for marketers to judge the efficacy of their campaigns.

S

Sales Qualified Leads (SQLs)

Leads that the sales department considers to be ready for follow up. Ideally, should be the same as MQLs, but a lack of proper alignment can lead to discrepancies in these metrics.

SEO

Search Engine Optimization, the process of ensuring that your website shows up at the top of as many relevant search results as possible.

SERP

Search Engine Result Page, the page that Google loads when you enter a search query.

Searcher Activity

Things that users do after typing in a query on Google. This includes what results they click on, what results they ignore, and what results they Pogo-Stick on.

Second-Party Distribution

Distribution channels that operate on sites you do not own, but where you have heavy influence on the listing. For example, Amazon.com.

Second-Party Media

Media channels that you do not own, but where you own the content you post. Examples include Medium, Facebook, and YouTube.

Site Architecture

The format of your website's data. A good site architecture allows search engines to easily index and crawl your website. This improves your search rankings.

Style Guide

This is your brand's holy text. This ranges from your brand's voice and what type of grammar you're expected to use all the way to how your logo and color palette can and can't be used.

Spam Filter

This is a filter used by email providers to weed out dangerous or overly-promotional messages.

Spam Score

This is a metric that some website graders use to determine the spamminess of your backlinks. Moz's Spam Score metric is the most reliable in my opinion.

Social Validation

This is a psychological trigger that encourages users to purchase your product because people like them have bought it in the past. This can be done with things like testimonials, reviews, videos, or social media.

T

Target Keyword

This is the word that you have identified as something that you want to rank for on search engines.

Third-Party Distribution
Distribution channels who re-sell your products, but give you little say in the presentation of your products, like a retail store.

Third-Party Media
Media channels that you do not own, who can do whatever they want with content you give them. This includes bylines and guest posts for magazines and blogs.

Top-Funnel
Prospects that aren't close to ready to buy. These are usually individuals who are just now learning about your product or service.

Top-Level Domain
The extension added to your domain name, i.e. .com, .net, .org, etc.

U

UI

The design of user interfaces for machines and software, such as computers, home appliances, mobile devices, and other electronic devices, with the focus on maximizing usability and the user experience.

UX Designer

A designer whose main focus is the user's experience, not how something looks.

UX

User experience. The process of enhancing user satisfaction with a product by improving the usability, accessibility, and pleasure provided in the interaction with the product.

Use Cases

Instances or reasons that a user would use your website, product, or service. For example, one use case for Facebook would be "connecting with friends from high school."

Visual Identity

How your brand identifies itself aesthetically. This includes your logo, color palette, iconography, textures, and photography.

W

Wireframe

A visual guide that represents the skeletal framework of a website.

www.ingramcontent.com/pod-product-compliance
Lightning Source LLC
Chambersburg PA
CBHW060251220326
41598CB00027B/4059